PASSPORT TO CAMBRIDGE CERTIFICATE IN ADVANCED ENGLISH

Practice Tests

PASSPORT TO CAMBRIDGE CERTIFICATE IN ADVANCED ENGLISH

Practice Tests

Jeremy Walenn

© Macmillan and English Language Arts 1990
© Illustrations Macmillan Publishers Ltd 1990

All rights reserved. No reproduction, copy or transmission of this publication may be made without written permission.

No paragraph of this publication may be reproduced, copied, or transmitted save with written permission or in accordance with the provisions of the Copyright, Designs and Patents Act 1988, or under the terms of any licence permitting limited copying issued by the Copyright Licensing Agency, 90 Tottenham Court Road, London W1P 9HE.

First published 1991
Revised edition 1992
Reprinted 1993

Published by MACMILLAN PUBLISHERS LIMITED
London and Basingstoke

ISBN 0 - 333 - 57984 - 4

Printed in Singapore

A catalogue record for this book is available from the British Library.

The publishers thank the following writers and publishers for their permission to publish texts in this book: The Sunday Times, The Daily Telegraph, Cosmopolitan UK Edition, Green Magazine, The Sunday Times A-Z of Preventative Medicine, The Time Inc Magazine Company, Auto-Express, 20/20, Family Circle, British Airways Highlife magazine, New Scientist (the weekly review of science and technology), Blaketon Hall Limited, Syndication International, Doris Kerris Quinn, Anne Karpf.

Design: Arc Design

Photographs and illustrations: Helen Ablitt, Zoe Ablitt, Chris Brown, Gina Kirby, Living Proof, Kate Palmer, Eleanor Pullen-Walenn, Richard Wileman, Josie Williams.

The publishers thank the following people and organisations for their permission to publish photographs in this book: Sally Koncki, Oasis Leisure Centre, S and I Williams Powerpix, Zanussi.

Contents

Introduction	6
Exam 1	
Paper 1 Reading	8
Paper 2 Writing	18
Paper 3 English in Use	22
Paper 4 Listening	26
Exam 2	
Paper 1 Reading	29
Paper 2 Writing	38
Paper 3 English in Use	41
Paper 4 Listening	46
Exam 3	
Paper 1 Reading	49
Paper 2 Writing	59
Paper 3 English in Use	62
Paper 4 Listening	67
Exam 4	
Paper 1 Reading	70
Paper 2 Writing	78
Paper 3 English in Use	81
Paper 4 Listening	86
Exam 5	
Paper 1 Reading	88
Paper 2 Writing	96
Paper 3 English in Use	99
Paper 4 Listening	104
Paper 5 Speaking	
Exam 1	107
Exam 2	111
Exam 3	115
Exam 4	119
Exam 5	123

Introduction

Who is this exam for?

The Cambridge Certificate in Advanced English is for people who need a high level of practical competence in English as a foreign language for use in the working world. You may already have a job or you may be starting a career, but if you need a high-level qualification in English for your work, then this exam is for you.

What does the exam consist of?

There are five papers:

Paper 1	Reading	1 hour
Paper 2	Writing	2 hours
Paper 3	English in Use	1½ hours
Paper 4	Listening	about 45 minutes, including 10 minutes to write the answers on the sheet provided.
Paper 5	Speaking	about 15 minutes

What is the pass mark?

To pass the exam, you have to get a grade A, B or C. Grades D and E are fail grades. You will receive details of your performance in each paper when you get your results. Each paper carries 20% of the marks.

What do I have to do in each paper?

In Paper 1, the reading exam, you have to read four texts and understand them in general and in detail. It therefore makes sure that you can read fast and effectively.

In Paper 2, the writing exam, you have to complete two writing tasks. The first is compulsory. You have to read various documents and then write, for example, a letter based on them. You then have to write another composition, and here you can choose one topic out of four. In both tasks, you should be able to write accurately and effectively, in a style and register appropriate to the context.

Paper 3 tests your knowledge of English in a wide variety of ways. You have to choose right answers, complete statements and correct pieces of written English. You also have to complete or expand a text, so showing that you can organise and produce written English suitable for a given purpose and type of reader.

Paper 4, the listening exam, makes sure that you can understand and act on spoken English. You have to listen to a cassette. A variety of tasks check your understanding of short and longer extracts of spoken English. At the end of the exam, you are allowed ten minutes to write out your answers on the sheet provided.

You take Paper 5, the speaking exam, with a partner. Each of you has an equal chance to express yourself while conversing in English about photographs and a topic. You need to be able to communicate with your partner accurately, effectively and reasonably fluently. There are two examiners present: one to listen and one to talk to you. You are being examined from the moment you enter the room. If you talk less than your partner, you will be given the chance to talk at the end of the exam, when the examiner who has been listening will talk to you. You will be marked for fluency and task completion, pronunciation, communicative ability and vocabulary.

Exam 1

Paper 1 Reading

Answer all questions.

Irradiation

Irradiation involves exposing food to a source of radioactivity and has the effect (depending on the 'dose' the food receives) of inhibiting the continued growth of the food (e.g. ripening of fruit or sprouting of potatoes) and killing micro-organisms and insect pests.

For the food industry it holds out the hope of a technical 'fix' which will allow fresh foods to be stored for long periods and will also sterilise the food. It has been promoted as a 'safe' and 'wholesome' process.

The main arguments against irradiation are:

a potential reduction of vitamin levels in food.
b it can mask the fact that food has been contaminated or is of poor quality.
c it can affect the flavour of food, especially fatty food.
d huge levels of irradiation may leave chemicals in the food.
e low levels of irradiation may create new kinds of micro-organisms.
f food inspectors have no test that they can use to check whether or not a particular food has been irradiated and so there is no way of checking whether a claim that an item has not been irradiated is true.

Questions 1 – 5

Below are some incomplete notes on the encyclopaedia entry 'Irradiation' above. Choose one word from the list of words in the box to complete each note. Write the correct number beside each appropriate word.

Note: You will not need to use all the words given.

1 Process: exposing of food to ...

2 Level of radioactivity that food is exposed to: ...

3 Purpose A: to stop food ...

4 Purpose B: to kill e.g. ... and caterpillars

5 Food industry wants to keep food ... and sterilise it.

☐ low ☐ variable ☐ bacteria ☐ ripe
☐ high ☐ irradiation ☐ fresh ☐ growing

Questions 6 – 11

These questions ask you to find examples of the six arguments 6 – 11 in the newspaper article. Beside each argument, write the number(s) of the paragraphs in which that argument is referred to. If it is not referred to, write 'X'.

Note: There are several answers in some cases.

☐ 6 There is a potential reduction of vitamin levels in food.

☐ 7 It can mask the fact that food has been contaminated or is of poor quality.

☐ 8 It can affect the flavour of food, especially fatty food.

☐ 9 High levels of irradiation may leave chemicals in the food.

☐ 10 Irradiation may create new kinds of micro-organisms.

☐ 11 Food inspectors have no test that they can use to check whether or not a particular food has been irradiated and so there is no way of checking whether a claim that an item has not been irradiated is true.

Irradiation – a step into the unknown

by Egon Ronay

1 The scientific position is that irradiation does not render food radioactive but it *is* accepted that an enormous number of molecular changes take place in the food as a result. Much of the argument is about the nature and consequences of these changes.

2 Innumerable new chemicals are initiated by irradiation. The nature of most is unknown or not fully known, but they are believed to include unstable molecules, known as free radicals, which may be further changed into a range of unknown and unstable chemicals. Oxidation of fats or lipids leads to free radical production and, because of this, fatty red meat and soft high-fat cheese are unsuitable for irradiation. There are reports that it would produce an unpleasant flavour.

3 The crucial question is whether irradiation could increase susceptibility to cancer. The Food and Drug Administration, America's official watchdog, says that the possibility of carcinogenicity is 'remote'. But one American researcher recently spoke for many sceptics when he described his Government's decision to allow irradiation as 'an extraordinary leap of faith'.

4 World interest followed experiments in India in 1975, which other scientists have been unable to discredit. Professor S. K. Srikantia, former director of India's National Institute of Nutrition, claimed to have seen potentially cancerous changes in malnourished children who had been fed stored irradiated wheat. This effect subsided after four weeks' storage.

5 Effects on hormonal regulation, among other adverse findings, were reported in a Japanese scientific paper and, in the USSR, irradiated bacon was found to cause cancer in the pituitary glands of animals. There are also reports suggesting that alfatoxin, a carcinogenic substance produced by moulds and linked with liver cancer, is produced in greater quantities in irradiated than in untreated food.

6 The International Atomic Energy Agency denies that irradiation, at doses approved by itself, can stimulate increased alfatoxin. But the uncertainties add up. Dr

Exam 1

Richard Piccioni, a senior scientist at the Accord Research and Education Association in New York, told a United States House of Representatives Committee in 1987: 'Scientific literature provides evidence to make a strong presumption of carcinogenicity in some, if not in all irradiated food.'

7 Dr George L. Tritsch from Rosewell Park Memorial Institute, a leading cancer centre in New York State, who has 33 years experience in cancer research, cited concern about 'free radicals'. He stated at a US Congressional hearing: 'It is completely irresponsible to proceed with the sale and distribution of irradiated food.'

8 As for the potential non-carcinogenic effects, the picture is very unclear. For example, irradiation inhibits both the sprouting and 'greening' of potatoes. The green colour indicates the presence of solanin, a possible miscarriage risk, but irradiation does not inhibit the production of solanin.

9 One important consequence not advertised by pro-irradiation scientists, is that irradiated foods are more susceptible to recontamination, for instance to infection by moulds and fungi, so that grains, fruits and vegetables may need post-irradiation fungicides. And, of course, irradiation kills useful bacilli, including the yeasts and moulds which fight botulinum.

10 We may be further lulled into believing that irradiated food is 'pure'. Richard Lacey, professor of medical microbiology at Leeds University, told me: 'The 10 per cent of listeria unaffected by irradiation can grow during the prolonged shelf life, even under refrigeration. When the food is sold, it could contain more listeria than before irradiation because the process removes most of the competing bacteria.' So irradiation can be counter-productive.

11 According to the outstanding paperback by Tony Webb and Dr Tim Lang (*Food Irradiation – the Facts*, Thorsons Publishing Group, £1.99), irradiation severely damages most vitamins. The loss of Vitamin C in fruit is 20 – 70 per cent; B1 losses in meat are 42 – 93 per cent and in some fish up to 90 per cent. Vitamin A losses in chicken are 53 – 95 per cent and 43 – 76 per cent in beef.

12 Scientists at the British Food Manufacturing Industries' Research Association at Leatherhead said that the vitamin loss 'does not matter because you get vitamins from other parts of the diet' which, to me, amounts to intellectual shoulder-shrugging. It is also nonsense to use the argument of prolonged shelf-life if irradiated food is more prone to subsequent recontamination and vitamin loss.

13 Much may depend upon the contamination of nearby food or how efficiently food is stored and handled. There could be a number of weak points in the contamination chain where organisms could flourish despite irradiation.

14 Taste, too, enters the argument. Irradiation, of course, stops ripening of fruit and vegetables, prevents its full nutritional value from developing and misleads our smell and taste mechanisms, which have been provided by nature to indicate what is good for us.

Questions 12 – 16

Below is a list of some of the organisations that have been doing research into the effects of irradiation. Indicate whether they are for or against the process by writing 'F' (for) or 'A' (against) beside each of them.

- [ ] 12 research centre in Russia
- [ ] 13 the British Food Manufacturing Industries' Research Association
- [ ] 14 the Indian National Institute of Nutrition
- [ ] 15 Leeds University, England
- [ ] 16 Rosewell Park Memorial Institute, USA

Questions 17 – 21

These questions ask you to consider the possible health risks for consumers on the basis of the information given in this article. Read the list of health problems below and decide whether they can or cannot be caused by eating irradiated food. Write 'Y' for 'Yes', 'N' for 'No' or 'M' for 'Maybe' beside each of them.

- [ ] 17 food poisoning (e.g. listeria)
- [ ] 18 miscarriage during pregnancy
- [ ] 19 cancer
- [ ] 20 lack of vitamins in our diet
- [ ] 21 radiation sickness

Exam 1

Man-eater

by Jocasta Shakespeare

1. On my first night in the jungle, there was an eclipse of the moon. The shadow came over it like the slow closing of an eye. The bush fell silent. No stars shone. A musty, honeyed smell from the mangroves wafted up the Ganges delta. Then the single alarm call of a deer broke through the blackness. A tiger was on the prowl. Monkeys chattered in fear, reached a clattering crescendo and then hushed. It was dead quiet. Then the repeated groans of a tiger, frustrated in his attempt to kill, made me hold my breath.

2. Ever since 1515, when the first recorded cyclone killed 200,000 people and tigers fed here on washed-up bodies, they have been addicted to salty human flesh. The local people are easy prey. They rely only on the blessings of Banabibi, the tiger goddess, to protect them. Her image, a doll clothed in white like a bandaged baby, sits in thatched temples which are dotted along the banks of the myriad creeks and rivers penetrating the forest. With her blessing, fishermen stretch their nets on mud flats at dusk, woodcutters bend double over their loads and honey collectors scale the short mangroves in the dark heart of the jungle.

3. Even out in their boats, fishermen are not safe. Six-hourly tides buckling back from the Bay of Bengal, where the sacred Ganges and Brahmaputra rivers meet, shift the tigers' territory, and so they have become expert swimmers, able to negotiate the creeks and channels. They use this skill to swim out to the boats of fishermen anchored from the shore to rest at midday, and steal a victim while they sleep.

4. When my guide grudgingly explained why dummies in the shape of humans were lying on the ground around the forest lodge, I was tempted to run away. They were the recent results of failed tiger aversion therapy. Models of woodcutters and fishermen were wired up to give the attacking tiger a sharp, but harmless, electric shock and dissuade it from repeating the experience. The discarded dolls, with back and head mangled, or arms and legs ripped away, show that attacks are nevertheless frequent and prolonged.

5. I didn't run away. I wanted to experience this delta jungle – a glimpse of the old wild India – before the tourist industry fills the more-visited reserves with tame elephants and half-tame tigers. To take a longboat out on a bright morning into the eerie wilderness of the mangrove swamps is to bring to life the solitary joy of the explorer Bernier who, in 1656, first described the Sundarbans to the West, or the stealth of the Portuguese pirates who used to hide their boats in these lagoons.

6. We headed straight for a curtain of tasselled greenery which suddenly gave way to a tiny inlet. On the banks, crocodiles smirked, basking in the sun; the mud on their backs dried to a grey-white coating and their pale lemon eyes glinting as we passed. Mangroves stuck their air-breathing roots out of the hot mud like bayonets. Mooring the boat, a heavily wire-netted passageway led to the foot of a watchtower. From the top we saw the dome of an ancient temple, entangled in wilderness, reaching to a sweeping curve of the horizon.

7. An open-bill stork alighted, wings sweeping the bush, and a black-capped kingfisher flashed into the foliage. On the edge of a water-hole beneath us, the square paw marks of a male tiger were pressed into the clay. We waited. For an hour the hot sun beat down and there was no movement. Not even the wind stirred. Then an unforgettable smell scorched my nostrils, lifted on the

convection currents from the ground below. A whiff of congealed blood and burnt hay – the smell of tiger.

8   And from the undergrowth round the stilts of the watchtower we saw him slink out to the water. There was no sound. His pads cushioned his weight. Just the light and shadow of his fiery stripes gliding over the mud. At the water-hole he crouched to drink, his back to us, and his bony haunches stuck out.

9   This was not one of the beautiful royal bengals which I had ogled from elephant-back at Kanha National Park in central India, while they panted in the effort of digesting an easy meal. This was an emaciated wild-eyed hunter and, when he turned to disappear silently into the forest, I thought I saw a manic stare in his yellow eyes. As we stepped gingerly round the netting and back to the boat, I hoped not to see those eyes again.

10 As we steered back through the waterways, dusk fell and, passing the watchtower, I saw the tiger's great temptation: a boatful of fishermen anchored at a 'safe' distance from the shore – all fast asleep, like dead people, lying at odd angles in the spicy glow of sunset. Remembering the hungry cat's eyes as he turned at noon from the water-hole, I hoped for their sake that he had already found his meal.

Questions 22 – 26

Below are a number of questions or unfinished statements about the text. You must choose the answer which you think fits best. Give one answer only to each question.

22 Tigers in the Ganges delta eat humans because
    a they are considered sacred, as they are protected by the tiger goddess.
    b they have inherited a taste for human flesh.
    c local fishermen and hunters catch the animals and fish they depend on for food.
    d they sense that man is their greatest enemy.

23 What does the writer think of the precautions taken by the local people?
    a They help to reduce the number of deaths.
    b They are simple but effective.
    c They do nothing to stop tigers attacking people.
    d They show how successful simple therapy techniques can be.

24 The writer wanted to go into the swamps by boat because she was
    a hoping to see a tiger.
    b interested in the history of the place.
    c attracted to a place untouched by tourism.
    d too frightened to stay at the forest lodge.

25 How did the writer know that a tiger was coming to the water hole?
    a She heard it moving through the undergrowth.
    b The birds flew away.
    c She saw its paw marks in the mud.
    d She smelt it.

26 What reminded the writer of the tiger on the way back home for supper?
    a The orange glow of the sun at sunset.
    b The colour of the light and the black shadows cast by the local fishermen.
    c The hungry look in the tiger's eyes.
    d Some local fishermen who had fallen asleep on their boat.

Exam 1

When did you last read a granny-bashing story?

by Anne Karpf

Have you noticed the speed with which new social problems seem to appear, then disappear? From one year to the next you never hear of child abuse, granny-bashing or drug addiction. Then suddenly, for months on end, they crop up in every newspaper, TV programme and government debate. And just as fast as they came, they go. Observers of social trends have a name for it: moral panic.

(27) ...

The objects of moral panics are often young – teddy boys, mods and rockers, Hell's Angels, skinheads, football hooligans, heroin addicts. They're also often female: there have been moral panics about surrogate mothers, abortion and the Pill (the moral crusaders couldn't resist the combination of young and female). (28) ...

Does it matter? After all, child abuse and AIDS *are* cause for concern. I'm not suggesting that moral panics are whipped up from nothing, but many of the things worried over have existed for some time. So why the sudden alarm?

(29) ...

And why that problem rather than this? Some 2,000 people die each year from asthma attacks, yet can you recall a single news report about death from asthma?

(30) ... They may actually help provoke the phenomena they condemn: some say drug abuse and violence increase after great media attention.

What should we do? As readers, we can stop buying the newspapers which peddle moral panics. We can protest at their easy outrage and moralising. (31) ...

Questions 27 – 31

In the passage on the left, some parts of the text have been removed. Match five of the parts of the text (A – F) below with the numbers (27 – 31) which indicate their positions in the passage. Note that one of the extracts below does not occur in the passage. Write the appropriate letter beside each number.

27 ....

28 ....

29 ....

30 ....

31 ....

A Take surrogate mothering, for instance. This has been practised, unregulated and unfretted over, for centuries but it was only in the Eighties that it produced a moral panic, leading to the Warnock Report which tried to control it.

B Moral panic was the name given by a British sociologist to those occasions when a condition or a group of people is suddenly identified as a threat to social values. Out come the editors, bishops and politicians to man the moral barricades, and the pundits ready with their diagnoses and solutions. After a while, the condition or group miraculously disappears, only to be swiftly replaced by another.

C Moral panics are far from harmless. They tell us what is deviant and they fan hatred. They bring phobias out of the closet. Moral panics about maternal deprivation make working mothers feel guilty.

D Statistics showed that the amount lost through fraud was roughly 100 times smaller than the amount of benefits unclaimed by those entitled to them.

E But, most significantly, they're branded as deviant, either because they're black (the moral panics over immigration and alleged black muggers), unemployed (the Seventies frenzy over dole scrounging), or gay (AIDS). Moral panics are never about bowler-hatted men or families with 2.4 children. They address a community of Us, under threat of disruption by Them.

F Above all, we can pause and question when a new cause for concern appears and the pundits move into action.

Exam 1

S'eau this is Perrier

by William Garner

1   At the Ritz Hotel, Piccadilly, London, raindrops sell at £2.35 a litre. Bottled, labelled and cellared, they appear on the hotel's wine list alongside Château Pétrus and Gevrey-Chambertin Les Cazetiers; ten different varieties from five different countries. 'We treat our mineral waters,' says Andrew Coy, food and beverage director, 'with the same respect as our wines' – which is no more than one would expect from an establishment where even the tap-water is served in a silver jug.

2   Silver jug or no, Ritz customers who prefer their raindrops in a form which hasn't passed through an estimated seven previous consumers – London area only: please check with your local Ritz – ask more often for Perrier than any other sparkling mineral water.

3   'I drink it because I like it, I really do,' said a friend over lunch. 'And you've got to admit, it *is* a smashing bottle.' That adjective raises another point: the Perrier bottle is glass, aqueous-green glass, elegantly unmistakable, all but irresistible with its chilled haze of condensation. A plastic bottle, even if it's blue and happens to be French, does lack that certain *je ne sais quoi*.

4   Looking at a glass of the world's best-selling sparkling mineral water – wine isn't the only drink with beaded bubbles winking at the brim – it is easy to imagine sylvan groves where cool, clear water gushes endlessly from the, well, bowels of the earth. Never mind whether the simile is indelicate. Is it true, or is it hype?

5   Evian is a product of Alpine rains and snows. Vittel rises among the wooded Vosges mountains. The waters of Vichy find their way into the valley of the Allier from the peaks of the Massif Central. Perrier? Anyone who has driven through western Provence during high summer won't need to be told that not even Julie Andrews would be able to evoke high peaks and flower-freckled pastures there. The only hills in sight are the Garrigues, a crouch of scrub-covered limestone behind the once-Roman city of Nimes: 300 feet is a peak in these parts. The southerly view is across the fertile but almost featureless plain that runs down to the salt marshes of the Camargue and the Gulf of Aigues Mortes (dead waters).

6   And sylvan groves? Any groves are a few feet high, ruled in straight lines, yielding soft fruit, wine grapes and early vegetables. Wind-lashed in winter, sun-battered by the time holiday-makers race over it to and from the Mediterranean coast, a good deal of the Perrier-yielding Vistrenque plain needs irrigation to get its crops to market. Flower-bowered Evian, nestling between Lake Geneva and the Alps, would never have thought to look there for a rival.

7   At the beginning of the 20th century the countryside which brings us Perrier was a land of Roman ruins, peasant farmers and oceans of undrinkable wine. So it could only have been the antiquities that brought Geoffrey St John Harmsworth, the youngest of three dynamic English brothers, to Vergèze, a village sitting only feet above the chalk ridges of the distinctly unscenic Costières du Gard.

8   In Vergèze he heard about a local curiosity, Les Bouillens, or bubbling waters, a cool, seething lake in which Hannibal is said to have refreshed his elephants and his army before his historic crossing of the Alps. St John Harmsworth went to see it and was impressed. Apart from perking up Hannibal and the Romans, it had been touted as a cure for half the ailments in the medical encyclopaedias, until Napoleon III and the law brought things under control in 1863.

9   Louis Perrier was a local French doctor with an interest in hydrotherapy and enough business instinct to lease Les Bouillens with an option to purchase. All he needed to switch the thrust from local spa to national market by bottling the bubbles was a backer. St John Harmsworth, sufficiently struck by the commercial prospects to invest, had both the grace and good sense to name the water after Louis Perrier. But it was he, with an English management, who sent Perrier water fizzing on its way not only through France but through the clubs and officers' messes of the whole British Empire.

10 Soon afterwards, St John Harmsworth paid a heavier price for his investment than mere money. Had a car accident not crippled him from the waist down, confining him to a wheelchair for the rest of his life, Perrier might still be just another effervescent spring water.

11 Never a man to give up, he exercised his arms and torso every day with the use of Indian clubs. At the same time, intent on making Perrier water a commercial proposition, he put his mind to the task of designing a truly distinctive bottle. In a world where high-tech exercise machines have turned the Indian club into a museum piece, it is useful to know that an Indian club was shaped like a wooden Perrier bottle, though today's bottle has slimmed down and boasts a more graceful neck. It was his concept not only to design the bottle, but to market Perrier as 'the champagne of table waters'.

12 Perrier was king. The name, if not necessarily the water, that came most frequently to the lips of those of us who could afford to buy something better than tap-water, rather than wondering, like much of the world, where to find drinkable water at all. Then disaster struck. A pollution scare made it disappear from the shops almost overnight. The British saying about a new monarch came to mind: 'The King is dead. Long live the King.'

Questions 32 – 40

Questions 32 – 40 ask you about the geographical features of various places mentioned in the text about Perrier water. The list A – J gives the various geographical features. Indicate your answers by choosing from the list A – J.

What are the geographical features of each place?

32 Evian *(2 answers)* ....   **A** mountainous
33 the Vosges *(2 answers)* ....   **B** hilly
34 the Massif Central *(2 answers)* ....   **C** flat
35 the Garrigues *(2 answers)* ....   **D** wooded
36 the Camargue *(2 answers)* ....   **E** fertile
37 the Vistrenque *(3 answers)* ....   **F** chalky
38 the Costières du Gard *(2 answers)* ....   **G** dry
39 Les Bouillens *(2 answers)* ....   **H** naturally irrigated
40 the Allier valley *(1 answer)*.....................   **I** marshy
        J windswept

Exam 1
Paper 2 Writing

Answer both Section A and Section B.

Section A

You are going to be in Britain for a month this year and are trying to plan a holiday there at the end of your trip. You have contacted a travel agency and have just received their plans for you. You are not sure that they are quite what you want.

Write a letter to them commenting on their plans and explaining what changes you would like made. Give any additional information they need.

Use their advertisement, your first letter to them and the questionnaire that you completed to help you construct your letter.

You may invent any necessary extra details to complete your answer (e.g. where you will be in the United Kingdom just before your holiday starts), provided that you do not change any of the information given.

You are advised to write about 250 words.

Ms P Collinson,
Tour Organiser,
Superhols,
37 Alexander Avenue,
London EC15 8TJ

26 February 1990

Dear Ms Collinson,

Thank you for your letter and the questionnaire, which I have completed and enclose with this letter.

As I explained to someone on the phone when I rang, I shall be in Britain when my holiday starts, so I do not need any help with my flight. That is already in hand. I do, however, need to get to Heathrow Airport for a flight at about midday on the last day of my holiday.

I look forward to receiving your suggested holiday plan and understand that I need to pay within thirty days of receipt of the plan in order to book my holiday.

Yours sincerely,

SUPERHOLS

The agency that designs a holiday just for YOU.
Holidays in England, Scotland and Wales to suit your interests and your purse.
For details, ring 01 284 5703 during office hours or write to Superhols, 37 Alexander Avenue, London EC15 8TJ.

QUESTIONNAIRE

Number of people on holiday: 1
Date of first day of holiday: 1 July
Date of last day of holiday: 22 July
Type of holiday required (please tick):
- ☐ tour by rail and taxi
- ☐ car tour staying in hotels
- ☐ car tour staying in inns and pubs
- ☐ one hotel, organised excursions
- ☐ self-catering

Place/Area(s) of interest (please tick):
Country: ☐ England   ☐ Scotland   ☐ Wales
Area(s) in England:
- ☐ London   ☐ south coast   ☐ East Anglia   ☐ south-west
- ☐ Lake District   ☐ Yorkshire & the Pennines

Area(s) in Scotland:
- ☐ Edinburgh   ☐ Glasgow   ☐ the west coast   ☐ the Lochs
- ☐ the east coast   ☐ the Highlands   ☐ the Islands

Area(s) in Wales:
- ☐ Cardiff and the south coast   ☐ the south-west   ☐ the west coast
- ☐ the mountains

Interests (please list):   Shakespeare, good food, good beaches for swimming and windsurfing, good entertainment facilities for the evenings

Budget (total amount of money available for this holiday in £ sterling):
£500

Special requirements (please list, if any):
room with a sea view and private bathroom please

Exam 1

YOUR SUPERHOLS HOLIDAY PLAN

Date of first day of holiday: 1 July
Date of last day of holiday: (21) July
Type of holiday: Hotel
Schedule:
Arrive: <u>Gatwick Airport 15.30</u>. Courier will meet you and take you to coach to take you to London.

1 – 2 July: Mayfair Hotel, Crescent Road, London W11. Organised sight-seeing, shopping and evening entertainment.

3 July: Courier will escort you to Paddington Station and travel with you by train to Exeter, Devon, and from there by car over Dartmoor to Torquay, a beautiful seaside resort on the south-west coast.

3 – 20 July: Hotel. You have a <u>room</u> with private bathroom in the Hotel Caroline, Cliff Road, Torquay, Devon. (See enclosed brochure.) This comfortable hotel is <u>within ten minutes of the beach</u> and has its own swimming pool, bar and disco. Torquay is a lively town and you will be able to eat fish in the many excellent pubs and restaurants and have the choice of the town's theatres, cinemas and clubs. Many interesting trips are possible. <u>If you wish to visit Stratford and go to see the Royal Shakespeare Company performing a play, please inform us.</u> We can arrange this, but you would be well advised to spend the night in Stratford, so we will book you a room on request.

(21) July: Our courier will escort you to a coach which will take you to <u>Gatwick</u> direct.

Check in time for return flight: 13.00
Total cost, including return airfares to Gatwick Airport and Agency fees: £495.95
Tickets and confirmation of hotel bookings etc. will be sent on receipt of the total sum due.

ENJOY YOUR HOLIDAY!

Handwritten annotations:
- A day early! See below too.
- Have arranged own flight. Not interested in London.
- Has room got sea view? No brochure enclosed.
- Yes please!
- Wrong day! No! My flight's from Heathrow.

Section B

Choose one of the following writing tasks. Your answer should follow exactly the instructions given. You are advised to write approximately 250 words.

1 Some English friends of yours are touring your country by car and are due to arrive at your house today to stay for a few days. You have just received an urgent phone call and have to go away for 48 hours. You leave a note on the door telling them to get the key from a neighbour. Write the note that you leave for them inside the house. Explain what has happened, apologise, tell them where their room is and give them all the information they need in order to make themselves at home. Warn them about any appliances they may have problems with and finally express your hope that they will still be there on your return.

2 An English businessman is going to come and work in your town. He is quite good at your language but needs practice and hasn't got time to go to classes. Write a letter giving suggestions and advice. Mention in your letter any films, books, newspapers or magazines that you would particularly recommend and why.

3 A lot of British tourists have been involved in car accidents in your area. Write a leaflet telling them what the dangers are, how to avoid them, and what the rules of the road are.

4 A great many British business people and residents in your country do not speak your language. Write an article for a local English newspaper or magazine giving your views on this and persuading them to learn the language.

Exam 1

Paper 3 English in Use

Answer all questions from Sections A, B and C.

Section A

1 *Read the article below and circle the letter next to the word which best fits each space. The first answer has been given as an example.*

A clean pair of wheels

Bicycles are the best means of transport ever invented. They are not only cheaper, cleaner and more (1) ... than cars. For a lot of us they are faster too. In fact, I was (2) ... how fast bicycles are two years ago when a van (3) ... a U-turn in front of me as I (4) ... head-down along Fleet Street. I (5) ... the side of the van at such a high (6) ... that my bike and I flew over its roof in a curve that (7) ... touched the tarmac twenty feet further down the road.
On the way to hospital I had (8) ... to reflect that, had I crashed into the side of the same van at (9) ... speed in, say, a car – or a horse – my (10) ... of being able to spring to my feet afterwards and swear fluently for ten minutes would have been remote. Bicycles, you see, are not just fast, but they are (11) ... .
Actually, it's not generally understood (12) ... how quick bicycles really are. Department of Transport figures show that the (13) ... speed of cars (urban and rural) driven over short (14) ... is 15 mph. The average bus speed is 8 mph and average rail speed is 16 mph. An (15) ... person can pedal a bicycle on the level at 10 mph; a fit person can pedal at 15 mph. So (16) ... on your bike!

(adapted from an article by Nick Crane in *Green Magazine*)

1 a amusement   b enjoyment   **c fun**   d entertainment
2 a remembered   b reminded   c thinking   d dreamt
3 a made   b took   c did   d gave
4 a pedalled   b pumped   c drove   d pushed
5 a crashed   b smashed   c hit   d banged
6 a acceleration   b velocity   c pace   d speed
7 a nearest   b next   c nearly   d nearby
8 a pause   b moment   c period   d time
9 a complete   b total   c full   d all
10 a opportunity   b chances   c occasion   d event
11 a safe   b secure   c sure   d dangerous
12 a even   b just   c still   d exact
13 a medium   b normally   c average   d everyday
14 a mileages   b distances   c journeys   d trips
15 a healthy   b sick   c unfit   d well
16 a mount   b climb   c get   d ride

2 *Complete the following article by writing the missing words in the spaces provided. Use only one word in each space.*

One of the best ways to unwind when you are feeling stressed is to have a massage. A gentle rub-down relaxes muscles, lowers your blood pressure and makes breathing slower and calmer. As (1) .... as making you feel relaxed, massage has other advantages. (2) .... example, because it relaxes muscles, it can relieve (3) .... (admittedly not many) kinds of pain. Headaches are frequently (4) .... by tension in the muscles of the face, neck and upper back. So, (5) .... you often suffer from headaches, it is probably (6) .... learning how to do it. You can make massage (7) .... of your everyday life by getting together with a friend and (8) .... how to do some of the basic techniques. Take one of the many short (9) .... now run, or buy a book, (10) .... sure it has clear directions and (11) .... of pictures. Some massage strokes (12) .... even be done without any oil, fully dressed. This kind of massage is a great (13) .... to relax and refresh busy friends. Why (14) .... learn a simple ten-minute back massage and then (15) .... it out on your family and friends?

Section B

3 *In lines 1 – 16, there is often an unnecessary word. It is either grammatically incorrect or does not fit in with the sense of the text. Read the text, put a line through each unnecessary word and then write the word in the space provided at the end of the line. Some lines are correct. Indicate these with a tick (✔) against the line number.*
In lines 17 – 25, there is often a word missing. Read the text, indicate where the word is missing and write it in the space provided. Indicate correct lines with a tick (✔).
In both sections the first two lines have been done as examples.

```
Dealing with the ups and downs of life is one of the most      1  ✔
difficult things to learn. On some hard occasions              2  hard
only the most stable personalities can cope, but it is         3  ...
these people who tend to be most successful in the life.       4  ...
On last Monday I was with a friend in her car, talking about   5  ...
her love life, when it burst into flames (her own car, not     6  ...
her love life). We next had to call the fire brigade. Was      7  ...
it all symbolic? Was someone trying to tell to her             8  ...
something? Her love life is pretty disastrous.                 9  ...
On Tuesday, her fridge exploded; on Wednesday then her         10 ...
television gave up the ghost. It's still only Thursday         11 ...
and yet she has just rung me. She hadn't closed the door of    12 ...
her washing machine properly so her kitchen had been being     13 ...
flooded. She was sitting on the floor beside her brand         14 ...
new machine in floods of tears. 'What else shall I do?'        15 ...
she asked. 'Get a mop,' I said.                                16 ...
```

Exam 1

```
'Believing that next week will be better the only      17  is
answer some weeks. Shaking a fist at the sky will only 18  ✓
give you tennis elbow.' She put the phone, but this    19  ...
is a good example of the argument. We cannot be happy  20  ...
all time, but this does not mean that we should be     21  ...
miserable day long either. A balanced attitude to      22  ...
the unpredictable experiences and events affect        23  ...
our lives is one of the keys success in our personal   24  ...
and professional lives.                                25  ...
```

4 *You are off to England by air this weekend. The friend you are going with has left this note on your desk. Read it and complete the formal information from your travel agent by writing the missing words in the spaces provided below. The first answer has been given. Use not more than two words in each space.*

You won't believe this! Take a deep breath!
All British airports are going to be out of action from midnight on Friday. The guys who handle the baggage on the carousels want more money or something. Apparently we could still go, though, as they are arranging other flights to Paris and Brussels. They'd take us by coach and boat from there. We would take a bit longer to get there, I reckon, as they won't tell us when we'll arrive, but no doubt we'll get there in the end. We can spend one night in Paris or Brussels if we want, too, and we don't have to pay for a room. As far as I remember, they take us all the way to London somewhere once we're in England.
Now that I've got used to the idea, it sounds quite fun. I reckon we should go anyway and spend a night in Paris if we can. What do you think? Give me a ring at home this evening because we've got to let them know what we want to do tomorrow.

We (1) ... to inform you that (2) ... will be no flights into British airports from midnight this Friday for the foreseeable (3) ... . Pay negotiations (4) ... airport management and the (5) ... union have broken down and a strike has (6) ... called from that time.
We have, (7) ..., made alternative (8) ... for all passengers who have already (9) ... seats on flights to Britain during the (10) ... in question. All flights will be (11) ... to Paris or Brussels, where it is our (12) ... to offer you a room in a hotel overnight. The following day you will continue your journey by road and sea to the (13) ... of your choice: Gatwick Airport, London Heathrow Airport, or central London.
We (14) ... for any inconvenience caused to passengers by circumstances beyond our control. Please complete the form below and send it back in the enclosed stamped addressed envelope by (15) ... .

1 *regret*   9 ....
2 ....   10 ....
3 ....   11 ....
4 ....   12 ....
5 ....   13 ....
6 ....   14 ....
7 ....   15 ....
8 ....

Section C

5 *Choose the best phrase or sentence to fill each of the blanks in the following text. Write one letter (A – G) in each of the numbered spaces. Two of the suggested answers do not fit at all.*

A as portrayed in *Dynasty* and *Working Girl*
B it is often observed
C although women often find it difficult to work for a man
D up 125 per cent
E even if not by design
F it has never been proved
G since men sometimes find it hard to work for a woman boss

Women, (1) ... , are better suited to entrepreneurial endeavour than the corporate culture with its masculine hierarchy and old boy networking. The latest figures released by the British Department of Employment show that over three quarters of a million women now own and run their own businesses, (2) ... , compared with only a 68 per cent rise in male entrepreneurs. And (3) ... , it is understandable that women-run businesses should attract other women – (4) ... . The Joan Collins/Sigourney Weaver-style boss, (5) ... , seems to be a male Hollywood scriptwriter's fantasy.

6 *You have prepared a telegram to send to the college you are going to attend in England. You are worried, however, that it sounds rather rude and so you decide to write a letter.*
You must use all the words in the same order as the telegram. You may add words and change the form of words where necessary. Look carefully at the example which has been done for you.

(a) CONCERNED AS NO RESPONSE TO PHONE CALL. (b) GRATEFUL ANSWER QUERIES. (c) DATE COURSE STARTS. (d) ADDRESS HOST FAMILY. (e) ARRIVING WEEK AFTER COURSE STARTS, PERSONAL REASONS. (f) PLEASE CONFIRM PLACE RESERVED. (g) ADVISE BOOKS TO READ BEFORE ARRIVAL.

a *I am rather concerned as I have had no response to my phone call.*
b ....
c ....
d ....
e ....
f ....
g ....

Exam 1

Paper 4 Listening

Answer all questions.

Section A First Part

Read the following information and questions 1 – 10. You will then hear the tape for the first part of Section A.

You are interested in taking a job as a tour guide for English tourists visiting your country. An English tour operator has come over to recruit guides and is giving a talk in your town. You are at the talk with the questions you have thought of in advance. You want to note down all the key information.
Study your questions.

Now listen to the talk. As you listen, complete your notes below with the answers to your questions and the details given.

1 Where Supertravel operates. Tick the correct box.

   ☐ **A** only in the UK   ☐ **B** only in Europe   ☐ **C** in most countries
   ☐ **D** in the north of England

2 Supertravel based in England – head office in ....

3 Types of tourist: under 25s: *if any, couples*

   　　　　　　　　　　26 – 40s: ...., *families*

   　　　　　　　　　　over 40s: ...., ...

4 Type of person they are looking for: *young, sociable,* ....
   ....

5 Qualifications needed: English language: ....
   Local knowledge: *attend course and pass test*

6 Supertravel courses: length: *1 week*   cost: ....

7 Length of tours: ....

8 Time of tours: ...., *summer*

9 Pay: .... *per* ....

10 Future job prospects: ....

26

Exam 1

Section A Second Part

Read the following information and look at the pictures 11 – 15. You will then hear the tape for the second part of Section A.

You have just bought a keep-fit course published in the form of a cassette and a booklet. The instructions are given on the cassette and, to help you do the exercises correctly, in the booklet there are two drawings of people doing each exercise. One person is doing the exercise correctly, the other is doing it wrong. Tick the correct drawing for each exercise.

Exam 1

Section B

You are going to hear an interview with Katrina Quinn, the Consumer Affairs Editor of the Good Home Guide, who will be discussing your rights when shopping. Complete the notes.

16 A contract is ....

17 The goods must be of merchantable quality, that is ....

18 The goods must also be:

   a ....

   b ....

19 A shopkeeper does not ....

20 If the price is marked wrongly the shopkeeper can either ....
    or ....

21 The shop must give you your money back if .... and even
    ....

22 When goods are sold privately, you must check ....

Section C

You are playing back the tape on your answerphone.

23 *Put these people in the order in which they left a message. Write a number 1 – 7 beside each of them.*

☐ **A** The landlord
☐ **B** The bank manager
☐ **C** A journalist
☐ **D** An employee
☐ **E** A friend
☐ **F** A neighbour
☐ **G** A relative

24 *Which of the people mention these things? In each space write one letter (A – G) from the list in Question 23.*

☐ A cheque
☐ Supper on Saturday at 8pm.
☐ Please ring back.
☐ Ill, please inform boss.
☐ Please feed cat.
☐ Arrange key on Tuesday.
☐ Returning call.

Exam 2

Paper 1 Reading

Answer all questions.

Communications systems

1 From smoke signals onwards, man's needs to collect and convey information has taken many forms. Heliographs, beacons, pigeons, lamps, semaphore systems ... now a many-thousand-year apprenticeship is climaxing in some of the most mind-spinning advances of all time. Modern information technology (IT) and the opportunities it presents are the results of hundreds of years of development. In particular, IT today has grown from two roots – telecommunications and information processing.

2 People have always developed ingenious ways of communicating with each other. But the big breakthrough came with the electric telegraph, launched in the late 1830s; and Bell's telephone, first demonstrated in 1876. Together they opened up the world to communication at a speed and distance that could only have been dreamed of before. But, by the 1860s, there was widespread appreciation of a communications system that was virtually instantaneous. A trans-Channel telegraph cable linking England and France had been laid in 1851. And, after several tragic and expensive failures, a Transatlantic link was finally completed in 1866. By then, the USA and Europe had set up national, linked networks communicating at a rate of 12 words per minute. And, by 1902, the telegraph encircled the globe. It was to remain in use well into the 1960s when it was superseded by the telephone.

3 Every time the telephone rings, we are audibly reminded of its inventor, Alexander Graham Bell. In fact, he was only one of several people experimenting with similar devices, but Bell was granted the first patent. A Scotsman working in Boston, Massachusetts, he tried for years to produce electrical signals from the tiny fluctuations in air pressure created by human speech. On March 10 1876, he finally succeeded in transmitting speech from one room to another.
Bell's telephone enjoyed almost immediate commercial success. Telephone exchanges were soon established to handle a growing network of telephone users. The unlikely figure of an American funeral parlour proprietor, Almon B. Strowger, made a major contribution to the continued success of the telephone. In 1891, tired of the inefficiencies of his local operators, he invented an electromechanical switch which opened the way for automated exchanges. His switches continued to operate the world's telephone exchange for over 60 years, only recently making way for electronic exchanges.

4 Until the turn of the century, telephone and telegraph were available only at the end of a cable. That changed in 1901 when Marconi made the first 'wireless' communication across the Atlantic. Used during the 1914-18 war, radio telephony made it possible in 1927 to talk by telephone across the Atlantic – if you could

Exam 2

afford $73 for three minutes. Radio telephony was the basis for global communications until 1956 when improvements in cable technology enabled the first transatlantic telephone cable to be laid. And in 1962, Telstar marked the beginning of satellite communications.

5   Since the advent of the telegraph and telephone – and, later the wireless and television – most developments in telecommunications have aimed at improving the quality, speed of transmissions, capacity and the sort of information that can be carried. The introduction of fibre optic cables has increased both the capacity and speed at which messages can be transmitted. The development of modems in the mid-1960s made it possible to convert digital information from computers into signals that could be transmitted through the telephone system. Today, with the increasing digitization of the telecommunications network, we can look forward to a system that will carry speech, data and pictures.

6   The other strand in the development of information technology is automated data-processing. Charles Babbage, a Cambridge mathematician, could be said to have almost invented the world's first computer. Between the early 1820s and his death in 1871, he worked on two types of machine: the Difference Engine, designed to calculate mathematical tables, and the Analytical Engine. Only a small part of the Analytical Engine was ever built. But Babbage defined the principles which would be realised by computers in the next century: that it should calculate, have a memory and choose its own computing sequence. Throughout the 1930s and 1940s researchers in centres around the world were developing the first computers. By 1950, 15 computers were either built or in construction around the world. A few years later, the computer was on the commercial market – to the fascination and alarm of a public that took some time to appreciate that computers are no more intelligent than what goes into them.

Questions 1 – 6

These questions ask you to choose the best title for each paragraph 1 – 6. The list A – I gives possible titles. Indicate the answer to each question by choosing a title from the list A – I.

What is the best title for each paragraph?

Paragraph	Possible Titles
1	A Over the air
2	B Vision and reality
3	C Processing information
4	D Switching to transistors
5	E Making connections
6	F Two technologies
	G From radio to rocket
	H Transmitting speech
	I Enter fibre, exit copper

Questions 7 – 10

These questions ask you to identify the technological developments A – G which relate specifically to the communication systems 7 – 10. Indicate your answers to each question by choosing from the list.
Note: Some questions may have more than one answer. The number of answers required is indicated after each question.

Technological developments

- **A** Satellite communications
- **B** Radio signals
- **C** Metal conductors
- **D** Digitization
- **E** Fibre optic cables
- **F** Automated data-processing
- **G** Electronic exchanges

Systems

7 Television *(1 answer)* ....

8 Telephone *(3 answers)* ....

9 Telegraph *(1 answer)* ....

10 Computer *(2 answers)* ....

Questions 11 – 14

These questions ask you to identify the systems A – E which have characteristics 11 – 14. Indicate your answers to each question by choosing from the list of systems A – E.
Note: Some questions have more than one answer. The number of answers required is indicated after each question.

- **A** Wireless
- **B** Telegraph
- **C** Satellite
- **D** Computer
- **E** Telephone

11 Which system does not use fibre optics? *(1 answer)* ....

12 Which system does not depend on cable? *(1 answer)* ....

13 Which system forms the basis of modern information technology? *(2 answers)* ....

14 Which system relies on changes in voice patterns? *(1 answer)* ....

Scanner hears the sound of wounded knees

The clunks and clicks of a torn knee cartilage are the key to a new knee scanner developed by a team at Queen's University, Belfast. The team were awarded the first prize in the Design Council's Toshiba Year of Invention competition for their new machine, which analyses the noises that a damaged knee makes to pinpoint the location and severity of the injury.

In very severe cases, torn cartilage can sometimes make a clicking sound that is audible to people standing nearby. The noise is thought to be caused by a sudden jerk as the tear disturbs the normal smooth movement of the bones in the leg.

Manual diagnosis by a skilled surgeon has an accuracy of only 60 – 70 per cent. This can be supplemented by X-rays or by arthroscopy, which entails surgically inserting an optic telescope into the knee joint. But these techniques are both costly and time-consuming.

To carry out the new technique, doctors attach three small microphones, known as accelerometers, to the sides of the knee and the knee cap. A goniometer, which measures angles, is also fitted. As the person bends and unbends the knee, clicks are detected by the accelerometers and fed into a computer. The form of the signals detected, along with the angle of the knee at the time, allow the doctor to assess the nature of the injury. The examination takes only five minutes and is estimated to be 86 per cent accurate.

Paul Maginn, an orthopaedic surgeon with the team, said that the researchers identified which noises relate to the tears in the cartilage by carrying out tests on patients who were about to undergo an arthroscopy and then comparing the results of the two tests. They are now working on incorporating routines for signal analysis into the computer software. These will automatically identify the characteristic clicks of torn cartilage from other background noise.

The new knee scanner will soon be subjected to a major clinical trial on several hundred patients. Maginn expects that two years further development is required before the machine will be ready to put on the market.

Questions 15 – 18

Look at the questions or unfinished statements about the text. You must choose the answer which you think fits best. Give one answer only to each question.

15 The new knee scanner
    a is able to X-ray the knee.
    b provides a manual diagnosis.
    c is used only in severe cases.
    d analyses sounds.

16 A goniometer
    a detects clicks made by the accelerometer.
    b operates when the person's leg is straight.
    c provides relevant data to assess the injury.
    d feeds signals into the computer.

17 This new technique for knee analysis
    a must be carried out by a skilled surgeon.
    b will always provide an accurate assessment.
    c is time-consuming to use.
    d may require other modifications before it is fully operational.

18 The noises made by a torn knee cartilage
    a can always be detected by a skilled surgeon.
    b are audible when the injured person stands still.
    c cannot be detected by a goniometer.
    d can be detected by arthroscopy.

Exam 2

A desert surprise

Off the beaten track in Namibia, Ros Drinkwater discovers a strange and beautiful land time has passed by.

'Wake up and come quickly,' whispered the Ovambo, shaking me gently. 'We think he is near.' I unpeeled my sleeping-bag and tiptoed across the sand. You could hear him crashing through the undergrowth on the far side of the water hole. Then he appeared, a huge desert elephant, ghostly pale in the moonlight. For half an hour we watched while he drank and munched *mopani*. Then he turned and vanished into the night.

Namibia, formerly South West Africa and due to become independent on March 21, has been described as a Third World country with a First World infrastructure. (19) ...

After the Bushmen came the Nama and the Damara, the farming Ovambos and the aristocratic Hereros. Over the centuries Europeans came and went. Only the Germans, fleeing a rapidly industrialising Europe, felt an affinity with the strange, arid land and in 1884 claimed it for the Kaiser. (20) ...

Close by is the ghost town of Kolmanskop, founded when an African literally stumbled on a diamond. After the discovery of the richer diamond grounds to the south, Kolmanskop was abandoned and its villas, shops and casino are sinking under the sands.

The appeal of Namibia is the sheer scale of its grandeur; the endless mountain vistas of the Fish River Canyon, the wide, flat Etosha Pan in the north, teeming with game, the Namib desert itself, which runs the full length of the coast and gives the country its name – at its centre a sea of apricot-coloured sand dunes towering nearly 1,000ft.

(21) ...

Swakop has a cosmopolitan air. It is popular with writers and artists and a favourite location for foreign film companies. There is excellent bathing and surfing, and miles of wide, sandy beaches – but take care near the harbour where the beach makes a sudden dive to the depths of the ocean and the force of the waves can knock you flat on your back.

There are several first-class hotels, but the Pension Schweitzerhouse, with the attached Café Anton, has a special charm. (22) ...

The ethnological treasures at Swakop's museum had whetted my appetite for a trip to the interior. The sea fog hung over Kaiser Street as we set off for Kaokoland in search of the nomadic Ovahimba tribe, who live much in the manner of their Stone Age ancestors. Kaokoland is not for the feeble. Travel is by four-wheel-drive vehicle only, and one vehicle travelling alone is not recommended in case of breakdown. Full supplies of petrol, water and food must be carried. My guide, Paul van der Bilh, is an expert in desert survival and a mine of unforgettable facts. Below are just a few of them.

(23) ...

At noon, the temperature soared to 40°C, at night we froze in our sleeping-bags. We made camp in dried-up river-beds mottled with leopard spoor, and drifted off to sleep counting the shooting stars, alert to the cries of hyena, jackal, and baboon; they were probably quite a way off but we slept with stout sticks by our sides in the sand, just in case. In the desert, you are always prepared.

Questions 19 – 23

In the passage on the left, some parts of the text have been removed. Match five of the parts of the text (A – F) below with the numbers (19 – 23) which indicate their positions in the passage. Note that one of these parts does not occur in the passage. Write the appropriate letter beside each number.

19 ....

20 ....

21 ....

22 ....

23 ....

A   But begin your journey gently at Swakopmund, the country's favourite resort, a bolt-hole for Namibians fleeing the summer heat of the interior. Swakop is a memorial to colonial town planning with wide boulevards and fine German buildings. Here the sun shines all year round, but at night cool fogs are blown in from the ocean, keeping the temperature at a comfortable 22°C.

B   Overseas visitors are often surprised by the excellent transport and communications, and the comparatively sophisticated life of the capital, Windhoek. But step off the beaten track and there is desert wilderness, unchanged since the Bushmen first settled it 3,000 years ago.

C   Stopping your car on the road is a criminal offence, but it is rumoured that more than a few of Namibia's 27 millionaires suffered vehicle breakdowns in this part of the world.

D   How to render a scorpion edible: remove the sting, boil it up and pretend it's a prawn. What to do should a black mamba crawl over you in the night: ignore it, the poor thing's just looking for warmth and if you can't handle that, carry a sealed tent. The correct mode of female dress for meeting the Ovahimba: preferably an ankle-length skirt, *never* trousers; the Ovahimba are gentle, but they have to draw the line somewhere.

E   They were a curious breed, those early pioneers, hardy beyond belief, but with a strong streak of romanticism. They trekked hundreds of miles in search of water, teams of 20 iron-shod oxen pulling their wagons, but where they finally came to rest they built Rhineland-style castles and art nouveau mansions lavishly furnished with the finest goods Europe could supply.

F   Its terrace is the hub of café society. It overlooks the town planners' *pièce de résistance,* a dual carriageway planted with palms leading from the centre of town down to the ocean. Some years ago, one end was sealed off. 'It was beginning to attract traffic,' was the cryptic explanation.

Exam 2

What's in a Face?

From ancient times, certain well-defined types of face have been invested with astrological significance and related to the Sun, Moon and Earth, or to the planets Mercury, Mars, Venus, Jupiter, Uranus, Saturn and Neptune.

The types are described below. They are familiar ones, though they may have passed unnoticed hitherto. The physiognomist soon learns that the people round about him can readily be grouped into a few classes, and, as his observation becomes keener and he assimilates the principles of the science, he finds the classes can be subdivided still further.

Again and again, he will be struck with the fact that in spite of the seemingly infinite variety in faces, there are some that are essentially very like each other. This physical likeness in unrelated persons is astonishing. Royal persons have their 'doubles', as have humbler individuals also. Are not a number of historical romances founded on a striking resemblance between one 'born in the purple' and another who saw the light in a peasant's hut? Folklore is full of tales of 'changelings' and 'doubles'.

To what degree does the physical resemblance indicate a similarity of character and attributes? Between persons of a like station the resemblance may be very close; in fact, it is sound practice for the physiognomist to ascribe like attributes to such individuals. In his readings of subjects, he builds up a fund of knowledge upon which he can draw for a quick interpretation of a person's features. Like the doctor, he learns from experience and applies his knowledge to new problems.

The well-marked types that we describe below are real ones, whether or not we accept the doctrine of planetary typology and its astrological significance. The latter theory is an interesting one, and it is remarkable that it has held credence for so many centuries.

Solar type. Tall or medium in height; rounded oval face, not too fleshy; complexion fresh; nose aquiline; fair hair; light eyes; leisurely walk and deliberate actions.

Lunar type. Stature medium to short; broad, rounded, fleshy face; pale complexion; bold, broad forehead; short, rounded nose; light brown hair; grey, moist eyes; action sometimes hesitant and undecided.

Mundane (Earthy) type. Broad, squat figure; prominent bones and squarish face; broad, prominent nose; strong jaws; hair and eyebrows thick and dark, the former growing low on forehead; dark eyes; action brisk but jerky.

Mercurial type. Tall and thin; face long and angularly oval; long, narrow forehead; dark hair; thin, long nose; eyes dark and sparkling; walk brisk and action smart.

Martian type. Neither tall nor short; strong, broad frame; facial framework square, but well rounded by muscular covering, and hence not angular; nose aquiline; hair generally fair or reddish; eyes green to hazel, bright and mobile.

Venusian type. Resembles the Lunar, but body is broader and not so tall, and face is more elliptical; hair brown; eyes also brown, or may be bluish; complexion clear; nose short and straight; action smart, and tripping walk.

Jupiterian type. Shortish, thick-set body, inclined to corpulence; face oval or hexagonal; forehead high and broad; hair mid-brown; eyes blue or brown; nose aquiline, fleshy; complexion fresh, reddish; walk stately and deliberate.

Uranian type. Tall and spare in build, conveying an impression of strength; face somewhat angular with rugged, bold features; hair dark; eyes dark and piercing; complexion pale or rather sallow; action brisk.

Saturnine type. Tall, thin; face long and angular; broad forehead; nose aquiline, prominent and bony; high and prominent cheek-bones; dark hair, sometimes black; sallow or pale complexion; gait slow, action deliberate.

Neptunian type. Somewhat short and lean; long, lean face; high forehead; fair hair; light eyes; action nervous; gait jerky.

Questions 24 – 27

Look at the drawings of the faces and from the information in the text identify the following types.

24 Lunar
25 Saturnine
26 Venusian
27 Mundane

A ....
B ....
C ....
D ....

Questions 28 – 35

Questions 28 – 35 ask you about the characteristics of different physiognomical types of face mentioned in the text. Items A – L list the characteristics. Answer each question (28 – 33) by choosing one item (A – L) from this list.

What are the characteristics of the following types of person?

28 The Solar type
29 The Mercurial type
30 The Martian type
31 The Jupiterian type
32 The Uranian type
33 The Neptunian type

34 What characteristics do the Lunar and Venusian faces have in common?
35 What characteristics have the Mundane and Jupiterian faces have in common?

A medium height and fairly thin
B short and stocky
C tall, looks strong
D movements uncertain
E distinctive nose and eyebrows
F bony face but not dark
G fleshy features
H bright eyes and quick movements
I thin face, nervous movements
J egg-shaped face, medium height
K fattish and round-faced
L medium height, wide shoulders

Exam 2

Paper 2 Writing

Answer both Section A and B.

Section A

You have recently applied for the job advertised below and completed the curriculum vitae as requested. The company has now sent you a letter asking for further information.
Reply to their letter giving the additional information they need and explaining why you think you are suitable for the job.
Use the handwritten notes which you have made on the letter, the job advertisement and the outline CV (which you do not need to complete) to help you construct the letter.
You may invent any necessary extra details to complete your answer (e.g. what you were doing between 1985-86), provided that you do not change any of the information given.
You are advised to write approximately 250 words.

CV (outline)

Name: ...

Address: ...

Age: ...

Education: Dates ...   School/College ...   Qualifications ...
            Dates ...   College ...   Qualifications ...

Experience: Dates ...   Employer ...   Position held ...
            Dates ...   Employer ...   Position held ...
            Dates ...   Employer ...   Position held ...

Interests: ....
....

Other relevant details to support application: ....
....
....
....
....

Exam 2

MARKET RESEARCHER

★ **RKO plc** ★

Required immediately. Good education and experience essential. Excellent salary for the right person.

Send full CV to
P.O. Box 99
RKO plc

★ RKO plc ★

Dear Applicant,

Thank you for your application for the post of market researcher which we have just received. We note from your CV that your experience in this field is <u>rather limited</u>. We did, however, find your application interesting and are willing to pursue it. However, to assist us we would be grateful if you could clarify certain points.

Firstly, there appears to be a break in employment between <u>1985 – 86</u>. What were you doing during this time? Secondly, you mention that you have acquired 'some' knowledge of computing and data processing but it is unclear <u>where this was gained</u>. Finally, the job of market researcher involves considerable contact with the general public and the ability to communicate sympathetically is vital. We note that you list as your interests: reading, bird-watching and playing video games. As these are somewhat <u>solitary hobbies</u> we wonder if they are a reflection of a personality that might not be best suited to this kind of work.

If you could provide us with further details on the points raised we are happy to consider your application favourably.

We look forward to hearing from you.

Yours sincerely

R Knight

Robin Knight

Handwritten annotations:
- 3 yrs !?
- Only 6 mths! Going round world – meeting a lot of people.
- Compulsory now at college!
- Relaxation when not working!

Exam 2

Section B

Choose one of the following writing tasks. Your answer should follow exactly the instructions given. You are advised to write approximately 250 words.

1 You have been asked to contribute to a magazine article about how marriage ceremonies vary in different countries. Write about how the event is celebrated in your country; include the preparations beforehand, the wedding customs and traditions and the party or reception afterwards. Add any other matters that might be of interest to the readers such as the clothes worn on the day, the special food and drink and the gifts that are given.

2 You have recently registered your house with a holiday exchange company. The idea is that you can spend your holiday in someone else's house, thus avoiding hotel bills and knowing that your own house will be occupied by the company's clients while you are away. You have been asked to write a full description of your property so that it can be matched with others. Include details of its situation, design, furnishings and any other features which make it attractive.

3 As part of a survey on emotions and feelings you have been asked to describe what makes you happy. You should include not only the factors within your control such as choosing your own entertainment or activities but also external influences like the weather, the actions and behaviour of other people and pleasurable events which occur by chance (meeting an old friend, finding a bargain etc).

4 The Museum of Modern Invention and Discovery has asked you to write a section for the English language version of its Visitors' Guide. They want you to describe the area of the museum displaying the latest advances in technology. The exhibits include not only items now in everyday use (computers, videos, etc.), but others which soon might be (videophones, pocket fax machines etc). There is also a special display of supposed technological advances which are now rarely used (laser discs, betamax video, 8-track stereo).

Exam 2

Paper 3 English in Use

Answer all questions from Sections A, B and C.

Section A

1 *Read the article below and circle the letter next to the word which best fits each space. The first answer has been given as an example.*

Australians have one big problem. Well, one in ... (1). Everyone thinks of kangaroos when their country ... (2) to mind. We all have an image from TV of them bouncing up and down, living a carefree ... (3). But, in fact, three million of them are killed each year. The reason? They are considered a great pest to one of the ... (4) of the Australian economy, sheep farming. The first settlers introduced sheep to Australia and since then they have thrived. Now the farmers are fighting a battle to ... (5) that the sheep have enough grass to eat and the kangaroos stay away from their land.
The Australian ... (6) is very dry. The land dries up and animals have to fight for the remaining ... (7) and water. A kangaroo with its ... (8) speed of 70 kph has the advantage over the sheep of finding fresh ... (9) ground. The kangaroo has always been a great survivor. Their life ... (10) is a sign of this. A baby kangaroo is born no bigger than the ... (11) of a peanut and climbs into his mother's pouch from the womb. The female kangaroo will then mate again and the ... (12) egg will remain dormant until the existing roo leaves the pouch. The female is then capable of ... (13) two types of milk; one concentrated for her roo in the pouch to help it develop and one less for the other roo. Adult roos will eat anything and can easily bound over the fences the farmers put up. During the hottest part of the day they will sleep in the ... (14) to keep their body temperature down, digging holes in the dust to lie in. Despite the Government sponsored kangaroo shooting, this ... (15) animal will survive.

 1 a principle   b principal   **c** particular   d main
 2 a brings   b goes   c think   d comes
 3 a exist   b live   c existence   d existing
 4 a founders   b finders   c foundations   d funds
 5 a make   b find   c insist   d ensure
 6 a forecast   b meteorology   c temperature   d climate
 7 a vegetable   b vegetarian   c vegan   d vegetation
 8 a high   b top   c above   d summit
 9 a chewing   b eating   c growing   d grazing
10 a circle   b cycle   c circuit   d circular
11 a make   b fit   c size   d round
12 a resulting   b coursing   c laying   d lying
13 a drinking   b inventing   c directing   d producing
14 a shed   b shade   c shadow   d sheen
15 a hardly   b hasty   c handy   d hardy

41

Exam 2

2 *Complete the following article by writing the missing words in the spaces provided. Use only one word for each space.*

Our temporary milk teeth are replaced by permanent teeth but if you have not looked after your first teeth .... (1) young you have only one more .... (2) to mend your ways. We would be lucky if our teeth continued to grow or were .... (3) more than once, as with some animals.

Have you ever woken to hear the persistent gnawing of rats and mice? The front teeth of rodents continue to grow .... (4) their lives. If we gnawed all day, our teeth would .... (5) away like those of the Inuit (Eskimo) women who softened animal pelts for clothing by .... (6) them.

Sharks have several .... (7) of teeth which are continually replaced. The shape of the teeth .... (8) between species, so if you want to check up on a shark's name, look inside its mouth!

Unlike bones, teeth don't often break. The hard part, mostly a form of the mineral calcium phosphate, is bound onto a flexible protein, so teeth are hard but not brittle. The outer enamel layer .... (9) about 97% mineral but the inner dentine layer has .... (10) more protein, about 30%.

Our mouths are .... (11) of bacteria, most of them harmless. But when surrounded by sticky organic material, these form a layer of plaque which causes the holes or dental cavities in our teeth. Hard tartar, which has to be .... (12) off with a sharp tool by your .... (13) is plaque with calcium salt deposits. If you don't clean your teeth well, food collects in grooves on the biting surfaces, ... (14) bacteria to collect and multiply. The acids, produced as waste by the bacteria, dissolve the mineral in the enamel. As the cavity gets bigger, ... (15) extends into the dentine, the hard inner substance of the tooth. That's when the toothache starts!

Section B

3 *In most lines of the following text there is one unnecessary word. It is either grammatically incorrect or does not fit in with the sense of the text. Read the text, put a line through each unnecessary word and then write the word in the space provided at the end of the line. Some lines are correct. Indicate these lines with a tick (✔) against the line number. The first two lines have been done as examples.*

Once humanity ~~has~~ lived in small groups where people of	**1** *has*
advanced age were revered. Their wisdom, gained through years	**2** ✔
of the experience, was recognised and put to the benefit of the	**3** ...
group. But society experienced a change and older people lost	**4** ...
their status themselves. Now that trend is in reverse. The	**5** ...

business community has been the first to witness the change. 6 ...
Because of following job shortages measures were developed to 7 ...
provide as many jobs for as many people as possible. One of such 8 ...
measure was the lowering of the retirement age. Now a 9 ...
considerable number of people in their fifties have been given the 10 ...
opportunity to stop work so that they can enjoy their leisure 11 ...
while then providing jobs for the younger generation. 12 ...

In this part of the question there is one word missing in some of the lines. Read the text, indicate where the word is missing and write it in the space provided. Some lines are correct. Indicate these lines with a tick (✔).

Last year Mrs Josephine Williams and family went⌐meet a long 13 *to*
lost brother at Heathrow airport. They took home⌐complete 14 *a*
stranger. Greatly relaxed by drinking on the plane, the traveller 15 ...
wandered the airport lounge to be greeted with kisses and 16 ...
cuddles by Mrs Williams and sisters. The family first suspected 17 ...
that something was wrong when their supposed relative tried to 18 ...
jump out their car on the way home. The man believed he was 19 ...
being kidnapped and was attempting escape. Mrs Williams said 20 ...
later, 'I thought the beginning he wasn't my brother but my 21 ...
sisters wouldn't listen.' 22 ...

4 *Read the following informal note which you have received from your flatmate. Using the information given, complete the advertisement at the top of the next page by writing the missing words in the spaces provided below. The first answer has been given as an example.*
Use not more than two words in each space.

Arthur,
Great news – I got that job in Spain but have to leave tomorrow. I must sell the car. Could you put an ad in the evening paper – I really need the money pretty quickly, so I'd better ask only £1,000 for it – I'll take a bit less but not much. Mention all the good points, excellent bodywork – no rust except where the wing's been bashed in. Amazing after ten years! Engine's in great shape but brakes need looking at. It's only got 65,000 on the clock – a lot less than usual. Don't forget to put that it's a sports car (MG) two seats, bright red – what everyone dreams of having!
Thanks for your help – 10% to you when it sells.
Terry
P.S. Try and get cash rather than a cheque – drop the price to get it if you have to. It shouldn't be too difficult to sell as I've really taken care of it all these years.

1 *sale*   8 ....
2 .... 9 ....
3 .... 10 ....
4 .... 11 ....
5 .... 12 ....
6 .... 13 ....
7 .... 14 ....

Exam 2

For (1) ...

A (2) ... year-old sports car (MG) in (3) ... . Below (4) ... mileage for the year. The car has been very (5) ... but the wings need some (6) ... . Very (7) ... engine but brakes (8) ... adjusting. This bright red two- (9) ... is a (10) ... at (11) ... £1,000 or (12) ... offer. There is a (13) ... if payment is made in cash. Phone today to purchase the car of your (14) ... .

Section C

5 *Choose the best phrase or sentence (given on the next page) to fill each of the blanks in the following text. Write one letter (A – G) in each of the numbered spaces. Two of the suggested answers do not fit at all.*

The fax of life

Once I borrowed a friend's house and the penance was that I had to sleep with a hamster. Hamsters, small furry animals, are boring creatures. They can't purr or fetch sticks like other pets. However, they do have one trick, which is to go round and round on a squeaky, rattly wheel. All night. Sometimes they might stop and refresh themselves by noisily eating or drinking, but mostly they tramp the wheel. What they don't do is sleep.

Whenever I think about getting a fax machine I remember the hamster wheel. Like a hamster wheel, the fax squeaks away both day and night; (1) ... . Once a fax is installed, snap goes the last holding link in the drawbridge that makes an English person's home his castle. Messages, chant the converted, can clatter out at you anytime of day or night.

(2) ... John Burt, the BBC news supremo, used to drive colleagues wild by sending fax messages to people two doors away. But Britain is still in an electronic Stone Age. In Hong Kong everyone carries personal phones that are as much part of their personal outfit as wristwatches and sunglasses.

What it is really supposed to guarantee, (3) ... , is freedom. But isn't there a trap in all this? Like the hamster wheel, the existence of all this electronic wizardry creates a desire to use it. Hamsters didn't evolve to use wheels. There are no known hamster wheels in the Mexican desert or the Ecuadorian jungles or wherever hamsters come from. Only once the wheel is given to them do they become obsessed with the compulsion to use it.

(4) ... , the important stuff got through anyway. They sent a runner the 26 miles from the battle of Marathon. The Aztec Empire sent runners too. Even the creation of a proper postal service did little to speed things up. Was anyone the worse off for the length of time it took to get the message?

Having said that, (5) ... and learn some new tricks for ignoring unwanted messages. Previous generations learned to leave the phone off the hook or pretend the gas bill had been eaten by the dog. If anyone asks me why I haven't replied to their fax I shall tell them it was accidentally shredded by the hamster taking a holiday from treading its wheel.

A the fundamental point of all this technological advance
B a restless reminder of the ceaseless activity of life
C notwithstanding the hamster's inability to sleep
D we have to rejoice in the advantages of instant communication
E the sound a fax machine makes may be disturbing
F Before we could communicate instantly
G The danger in this is letting it go to your head.

6 *Your secretary has taken down a message for the Managing Director. As her personal assistant, you will need to rewrite it in an acceptable form. You must use all the words in the same order as the notes. You may add or change the form of the words where necessary. Look carefully at the example.*

A anxious discuss proposed purchase (shop)
B like to arrange meeting Thurs. approx. 2pm
C not convenient suggest Fri. morning 9 sharp – v. busy man
D requests meeting – his office
E info. required on latest profits/costings etc.
F good chance contract with Harold Bros.
G important move quickly – time short

To: Ms Ducan (MD)
From: Mr Michael Coleman (PA)

Sir,
My secretary received a telephone call from Mr Rowboat at Rowlon plc which requires immediate attention. Below I summarise the important points.

A *He is anxious to discuss the proposed purchase of the shop.*
B ....
C ....
D ....
E ....
F ....
G ....

I shall be available all afternoon should you need me.

Michael Coleman

Exam 2

Paper 4 Listening

Section A First Part

Two colleagues will be travelling by train today; one going from Oxford to London for a meeting, the other from Oxford to Heathrow to catch the 11.30 flight for Paris. On the radio you hear that there are problems on the Oxford to Paddington line. You phone British Rail to get the latest travel information. You note down some of the details but need to listen again to make sure you have heard the information correctly. You wish to contact your colleagues and tell them exactly what the situation is so that they can change their plans if necessary.

1 Services subject to ....
   following an earlier collision.

2 Near where did the train leave the line?
   ☐ A ☐ B ☐ C ☐ D ☐ E ☐ F

3 Where was the passenger train coming from?
   ☐ A ☐ B ☐ C ☐ D ☐ E ☐ F

4 From which town are trains late or cancelled?
   ☐ A ☐ B ☐ C ☐ D ☐ E ☐ F

5 How many trains an hour are there from
   Swindon to London? ....

6 Advice given for passengers wishing to go to Heathrow:
   ....

7 Advice given for passengers bound for High Wycombe:
   ....

8 Can passengers get a refund if they wish?   ☐ Yes   ☐ No

Section A Second Part

You have decided to go to the cinema this evening with a group of friends and phone a recorded service which gives details of all the films showing at the three-screen complex.
As all your friends have different tastes, you need to have sufficient information to be able to reach a compromise. Note down the following information.

	Time(s)	Film Title(s)
9 Screen 1:	....	....
10 Screen 2:	....	....
11 Screen 3:	....	....

Type(s) of Film

12 Screen 1: ....
13 Screen 2: ....
14 Screen 3: ....

Section B

You are going to hear an interview with an expert on accident prevention on aspects of safety and the steps we can take to make our lives safer. Complete the notes.

15 Safety is a matter of ....
    ....
    ....

16 One of the most likely places to have an accident is ....
    ....

17 Two causes of these accidents:

   a ....

   b ....

18 In the event of being burnt you should ...., but in no circumstances should you ....

19 Generally safe forms of transport are .... and ....
    The most dangerous is ....

20 Two hidden dangers in the garden are ....
    and ....

21 Most accidents are avoidable if ....

22 The expert's worst experience was ....

Section C

You are going to hear a number of people making suggestions on ways in which our environment can be improved.
Question 23 lists the people who speak on the tape. Put them in order 1 – 7.
Question 24 lists the suggestions they make. Match the suggestions to the people. Write a letter A – G beside each suggestion.

23 *Put the following people into the order in which they speak.*

☐ A   a non-smoker   ☐ E   a park-keeper
☐ B   a conservationist   ☐ F   a scientist
☐ C   a mother   ☐ G   a politician
☐ D   a businesswoman

24 *Which of the people suggests these things?*

☐   recycling products   ☐   planting more trees
☐   reducing the number of cars   ☐   cutting energy consumption
☐   controlling litter   ☐   protecting wildlife
☐   banning smoking in public places

Exam 3

Paper 1 Reading

Answer all questions.

Green housing

Roger Dean and David Huw Stephens are experts in architecture and design, working for harmony of design and style with green consciousness. The Findhorn Foundation is building an environmentally friendly village. Janet Angus reports:

1   The current climate of 'environmental awareness' has at last opened up possibilities for architects who for years have striven to radically change the way buildings are conceived. Demand for housing, particularly in over-populated areas such as the South of England, has allowed poor building practices to gain a stranglehold on what is, after all, one of the most important purchases anyone is likely to make in a lifetime. Barely a thought is spared for the comfort or even practical requirements of the family today. More important is to make a fast buck, using the cheapest, easiest and quickest materials, moving smartly on to the next job and its associated profit. Needless to say, not all architects are tarred with this brush but those in dissent have had a hard time of it getting their small voices heard.

2   These enlightened ones have been working on a number of key issues. These are namely the needs of a family, with particular reference to privacy and security, safety, energy conservation, waste control, natural air conditioning, practical and enjoyable space. Their houses for the future will have the ability to blend into or complement their surroundings and be constructed of environmentally acceptable materials. They will also employ environmentally sound appliances. Throwing conventional building design to the wind, the most striking feature of the Home for Life is the globoid design of the rooms. The result of research into the most comfortable, safe, secure shaped space for human beings to inhabit, the curved 'walls' have the added benefit of recirculating warm air round the room. This deflection results in tremendous energy savings as two people or a single light bulb is sufficient to heat a room.

3   Turning their backs on bricks and mortar, the Deans construct their shapes by spraying gunnite onto moulds under extreme pressure. Taking a mere three days to cure, the process is quick and simple. The ovoid shape makes it structurally very strong. Gunnite is also a good insulator – again saving on energy costs. The outside of the buildings may be decorated in any way desired. Burying much of a house would not only act as a good insulator but would also help it to blend into the landscape. Natural air conditioning works by storing water in open jars in the basement, the air rising through parallel vents and circulating round the house. Solar power is to be incorporated although Roger Dean is not convinced that the technology for collecting it is as yet sufficiently developed. Attention to details such as the complete elimination of sharp corners internally makes the

house safer for children and clumsy adults too. Kitchen appliances will utilise hydrogen gas which is considered safer than natural gas as its effluent is water. Slightly more expensive, this can be weighed up against the safety aspect.

4   Building scientist David Huw Stephens has taken a slightly more conventional approach in that his solar village, currently under construction in Rhayader, mid-Wales, retains the rectangular 'house shape' we are used to. His crusade began ten years ago but it is only now that the market has been sufficient to enable the project to at last get under way. With the encouragement and support of Radnor District Council, a village comprising ninety houses is being constructed. The designs are more conventional in that the rooms are the more familiar box shapes. Building materials, however, demonstrate a great deal of consideration of environmental logic. Brick has been rejected on the grounds that it contributes nothing to thermal insulation. Water on brick has the same effect as when your hair is wet after washing, i.e. you feel cold. These walls, therefore, are clad externally in Welsh slate which shed water as a liquid rather than evaporating it off. Heat loss is dependent on the difference between the temperatures inside and out. If the outside is wet, it has the effect of lowering the temperature 15 – 20 per cent.

5   The houses are passive solar buildings. This means that the building itself acts as a solar collector. The village is built on a south-facing slope and the entire south facade of each building is double or triple glazed Scandinavian softwood windows. Built with a steel frame, the houses are extremely strong (hurricane resistant). This also allows the walls to incorporate 20cm of insulation – more than twice that required by building regulations. As the frame spans the entire width of the house, it is possible to use the internal space any way you like. Quite apart from the traditional energy saving methods of insulation and draft exclusion, Stephens has implemented some extremely simple but effective ideas such as having the living accommodation on the first floor and sleeping downstairs. Heat rises, it is therefore only a question of logic. Yes, heat rises, up through the first floor and into the roof space which is usually a tremendous source of wasted energy. Stephens' houses incorporate a greenhouse on the roof which will absorb all the heat you care to feed it. Not only is this a better way of using normally wasted space but it provides a winter garden, enabling you to grow your own food. This will obviously save you money but it also means less demand for juggernauts hurtling across the continent with your food requirements. Triple glazing is employed. This is better than conventional double glazing which simply seals a house up and causes condensation problems. A passive ventilation system, these windows allow the air coming in between the panes to rise up to the greenhouse and finally escape through there, again putting wasted heat to good use.
All these factors add up to a house which requires very little topping up heat. Heating bills would typically be £30 per annum, a saving of about 90 per cent.

Exam 3

Questions 1 – 5

These questions ask you to choose the best title for each paragraph 1 – 5. The list A – H gives the possible titles. Answer each question by choosing from the list. What is the best title for each paragraph?

Paragraph

1 ....

2 ....

3 ....

4 ....

5 ....

Possible title

A A scientifically built village
B Interior and exterior design
C Environmentally-friendly materials
D Energy efficiency
E The greenhouse effect
F Homes to suit a family's needs
G The housing market
H Building restoration

Questions 6 – 10

These questions ask you to identify certain advantages. The list A – G gives the various advantages. Indicate your answers to each question from the list A – G. Some questions have more than one answer.
What are the advantages of the following when building houses?

6 curved walls *(3 answers)* ....
7 gunnite *(2 answers)* ....
8 steel frame *(3 answers)* ....
9 Welsh slate *(2 answers)* ....
10 hydrogen gas *(2 answers)* ....

A good insulation
B water resistant
C energy saving
D safer
E cleaner
F cheaper
G space-saving

Questions 11 – 14

These questions ask you about the factors involved in modern building. They are listed in A – F. Indicate your answers by choosing from this list.

11 What factors contribute to wasted energy? *(2 answers)* ....

12 What factors contribute to heat loss? *(2 answers)* ....

13 What factor contributes to wasted space? *(1 answer)* ....

14 What factors are beneficial to the environment? *(2 answers)* ....

A brick walls
B roof space
C double glazing
D greenhouses
E natural gas
F solar collectors

51

Exam 3

The art of teaching art

Why a remote rural school has won 2,000 prizes and awards, by Jay Branegan

Sangkom Thongmee, 37, is a $240-a-month art teacher at a rural secondary school in north-east Thailand, the country's poorest region. He scrounges for pencils and paint, often paying for them himself. His students, most of them farmers' children, sit and work on the bare floor because there are no funds for chairs or desks in his classroom. For an assignment, he sometimes has them make paper mosaics by cutting up old magazines. 'It saves money,' he says. But Sangkom is unlimited in his gifts as a teacher. And so he has attracted the attention of the outside world.

Every Thursday night, Sangkom climbs onto a bus in his hometown, Wangsaphung, for the overnight journey to Bangkok. After a jangling nine-hour ride, he arrives at dawn and makes his way to Chitralada Palace, the sprawling residential compound of the Thai royal family. There, for six hours, he becomes a visiting art instructor at the Chitralada School, where young princes, princesses and other children of the royal household study drawing and painting under his guidance.

The surroundings and the resources are a teacher's dream. But as soon as his palace labours are done, the long-haired Sangkom leaves the glittering city to return to Room 211 at the remote Sri Songkram Wittaya high school outside the provincial capital of Loei. He has taught there for his entire twelve-year career, despite many offers to go elsewhere. 'My duty is here,' says the intense but soft-spoken Sangkom. 'In my small world, if I can see these kids get an opportunity to practise and enjoy art, that's enough.'

The royal interest in the up-country schoolteacher is only a few months old. But his fame has been spreading for longer than that. Soon after Sangkom arrived at Sri Songkram in 1978, following his graduation from Chulalongkorn University in Bangkok, his students started winning awards in all sorts of art competitions. From that beginning, Sangkom's pupils have gone on to accumulate more than 2,000 prizes and other awards. Last year, for instance, one student won a poster design contest at an international AIDS conference in Montreal, while another took first place in a Chinese government-sponsored painting competition on the environment.

The prizes themselves are not important, says Sangkom, 'but they show that kids from rural areas can be creative through art, if only they have someone to pull them along. City children may be more expressive, but not necessarily more creative. Once I get my students to open up, they are often able to put more feeling into their paintings.'

Questions 15 – 19

Look at the questions or unfinished statements about the text. You must choose the answer which you think fits best. Give one answer only to each question.

15 The teacher
 a receives funds from the farmers.
 b makes his pupils sit on the floor.
 c works mainly in the city.
 d often has to borrow equipment.

16 The passage suggests that teaching the royal children is
 a the teacher's dream.
 b difficult because there are few resources.
 c a laborious job.
 d not what the teacher really wants to do.

17 The passage implies that
 a the teacher is personally ambitious.
 b the children are born artists.
 c the children are able to fulfil their artistic potential.
 d few people know what Sangkom is doing.

18 The students enter art competitions
 a to try and win money.
 b when they have graduated from university.
 c to try to become famous.
 d as a way of developing creativity.

19 The main purpose of this article is to
 a profile the life and work of a famous artist.
 b contrast rural life and city life in Thailand.
 c examine the relationship between the art teacher and the royal family.
 d show what can be achieved in less than ideal circumstances.

Exam 3

A life in the day of Anita Roddick

Anita Roddick, founder of the Body Shop, talks to William Foster.

I start the day in a good mood. I'm always delighted to wake up still alive. I need a few moments to adjust to this discovery and relish the only self-indulgent bit of the day. Gordon gets up first at seven. Neither of us can bear breakfast in bed; even lounging in the bath is a bit repellant. So I'm in and out of the shower even faster than he is. Then comes the next brief pause of the day, which is deciding what to wear. It always comes to jeans and a T-shirt, plus a tweedy jacket for an important meeting.

Breakfast is always Greek yoghurt, fruit and coffee and I never leave for the office without chatting to Julian, our punk rock gardener, who's an absolute treasure. We have a lovely house on the South Downs, which used to belong to Arthur Rackham, the artist. I don't know what he'd think of our additions to the garden, which include plastic jumping fish, and glass fibre cows looking over the hedge.

(20) ...

I'm always being asked what I put on my face in the morning, as if we're into beauty preparations, which we're not. Our way is to unearth the simple substances women the world over have used to groom themselves for centuries.

A lot of what I do is to stimulate ideas. Gordon's job is to oversee the finances and keep my feet reasonably near the ground. (21) ...

I set up my own training school in London. I have my own film and video group. If it's a London day, I use the Tube rather than hired cars because I'm terrified of the fat cat mentality. You get out of touch that way.

Now and again I escape with the family to our house in Scotland to do a bit of walking and toast ourselves in front of huge log fires. (22) ...

I started off as a teacher, then got a job with the United Nations in Geneva, making so much tax-free money that I gave it all up and boogied off round the world for a year. (23) ...

Gordon was a penniless poet when we married. It was in Reno. While I was in the States, I saw a car repair place called the Body Shop. I thought how wonderful it would be if you could buy products for your hair and skin in small amounts.

In the end, I went to see the manager of Barclays Bank in Littlehampton and borrowed £4000 for the first shop. (24) ... The elderflower cream had pips in it and there were bits of cucumber in the cleansing milk. But nobody minded and we took £130 on the first day.

Exam 3

Questions 20 – 24

In the passage on the left, some parts of the text have been removed. Match five of the parts of the text (A–F) with the numbers (20–24) which indicate their positions in the passage. Note that one of these parts does not occur in the passage. Write the appropriate letter beside each number.

20 ....

21 ....

22 ....

23 ....

24 ....

A I talk all day, goading on the staff, asking questions and keeping the company breathless and motivated. I pause for a mid-morning coffee and a sandwich for lunch, washed down with ice-cold water and camomile tea. If I'm hungry, I steal Gordon's apple or raid the staff's biscuit tins.

B Otherwise, we're not awfully good at taking holidays. My parents came from Italy to settle in Littlehampton and ran a café. But my father died when I was ten, so we four kids always worked. We never had holidays.

C Rain came through the roof so I covered the walls with garden lattice and painted the rest green. We had fifteen herbal creams and shampoos for sale, all in plastic bottles, with labels hand-written by me.

D When I was in Tahiti, I watched the Polynesian women plastering themselves with what looked like great lumps of lard. This turned out to be untreated cocoa butter. Now we buy more cocoa butter than any other importer.

E But I knew it might be something special when I discovered the American Navy had been stockpiling it since 1945 to use against the side-effects of radiation.

F It's only 15 minutes down the road to the office. If it's Saturday, Gordon may be playing polo at nearby Cowdray Park but I go to the office to phone, to write, to glean ideas and pick up those wonderful smells of flowers and fruit that go into our products. The Rover Sterling I drive has been converted to lead-free petrol but they can't do much about Gordon's five-year-old Jaguar, so the sooner he changes it the better.

Exam 3

File-Safe Systems

Matt Coward offers light-hearted advice to workplace eco-rebels. Stan Eales draws his own conclusions.

For the most environmentally conscious workers, life at the office, shop or factory is still that of a guerrilla, trapped behind enemy lines, carrying out a slow war of attrition against outdated ideas and habits. What follows is an incomplete guide to action for the eco-friendly – the employee who is tired of waiting for the bosses to change their ways, and decides to give a few reminders.

First, a word about absenteeism. For the dedicated idler, it is encouraging to realise that sloth is becoming a revolutionary act. The common cold has always been nature's way of telling you that you don't fancy going in today, but as the ecological crisis deepens, the 'worker's awayday' is a highly responsible answer to the problem of pointless work.

The jobs that most of us do are unnecessary. (This doesn't apply to magazine writers, of course.) To put it bluntly, if you are Something in the City, your best bet for saving the planet is to stay at home. In this daft, unnatural world, a frightening proportion of working hours are spent using up scarce resources, and producing absolutely nothing but money and waste. Stockbrokers and estate agents are a luxury we can no longer afford.

Stationery

Less is the key word here. It's all very well switching to recycled paper, but Britain uses 130 million trees-worth of pulp every year and overall consumption just has to drop. Meanwhile, there really is no good excuse for not using the recycled stuff – quality and availability have improved enormously in recent years. If, due perhaps to some undiagnosed personality defect, your boss is still reluctant to make the change, just do it yourself. Re-use every scrap. For instance, write a letter to his tax inspector on the back of one he's received from his accountant. He'll soon come round to your way of thinking.

As a rule of thumb, avoid anything with 'disposable' in its name. A relatively harmless alternative to the plastic biro might be a quill pen – thought it could hardly be described as cruelty-free. Pencils are favourite, not least because they break so often you never have to do any actual writing with them. Fountain pens are another alternative or, if you want something disposable, try the Jet Pen which is made from biodegradable cardboard (by order from Danny Pollock Promotions of London).

Photocopiers are about as green as Daleks. Not only do they gulp down gallons of vile chemicals faster than a yuppie drinks blood, but they aren't keen on recycled paper. Actual sabotage of these machines is, however, usually unnecessary. Left to their own devices they can be relied upon to break down every ten minutes anyway. Simply unplugging the photocopier is all the subversive employee need do – just remember you'll have to switch it back on when you want to run off a copy of your 800-page green novel during the lunch break.

Transport

Of all energy used in Britain, 20% goes on transport.

But can you see your supervisor on a bicycle? Next to walking, it's the most ecologically sound way of getting to work, and if the directors miss their status symbols, they could always try painting a Silver Lady on their mudguards.

If they insist on keeping their motors, suggest a car-pool. If they turn that down, start operating an informal pool – turn up at your employer's house on Monday morning and wait in the back seat.

Lead-free petrol and catalytic converters only help with one of the problems caused by cars – exhaust pollution – but it's a step forward at least. Some people still fear a loss of power from changing to lead-free, but with urban speeds averaging around 11 m.p.h. the ability to go at twice the legal limit is a dubious advantage anyway.

One word of warning: if you conspire to replace your firm's fleet of vans with rickshaws, someone's going to have to pull them – and it isn't going to be the guv'nor.

The Building

Working at home (as opposed to just skiving at home) is a way of saving on transport costs, spreading population density, and giving property speculators less excuse for sticking office blocks all over the Green Belt. On the other hand (the expression with which environmentalists seem to begin every other sentence), it must be more economical to use communal facilities, in a central workplace, than duplicating them in their own home.

Health

Most offices make you ill, and not just because you have to share them with dull, overpaid drones who don't appreciate you properly. Air-conditioning, fluorescent lighting and VDUs all contribute to health hazards. Use an ioniser to replace the negative ions which electrical equipment destroys.

Canteen

Your works canteen or restaurant should only be serving organic food with vegan and vegetarian options. Quite apart from the damage inorganic pesticides and fertilisers do to the environment and to human bodies, they are a dreadful waste of money. Farmers in the UK spend nine million pounds a year on slug pellets alone, and they don't even work. All that happens when a pest is killed, is that its predators die off too. So next season, you've got a fresh load of fast-breeding pests with no natural enemies.

Make a fuss about the source of works food. To say you've been off sick because of inorganic apples (sprayed with 20 substances, including the suspected carcinogen Alar) is a neat trick. Or invite a cute little baa-lamb to lunch when one of his cousins is on the menu. Most carnivores are superstitious, sentimental souls, and will rush out of the dining room looking sheepish.

Try growing your own lunch on the office windowsill, or in the wasteland where the car park used to be (see Transport, above). Seeds for sprouting are available from seedsmen's catalogues, and provide the most vitamin-rich food possible, since the young plants are actually still growing at the moment you crunch into them. (Yes, it's sad, but try not to think about it.) Put the seeds into a jar covered with muslin, rinse them twice a day, and use them when their tails start wagging.

To discourage the buying of disposable paper cups, fashion them into representations of management and stick them on poles in the entrance lobby.

Exam 3

Questions 25 – 34

Answer these questions by referring to the article File-Safe Systems. Questions 25 – 34 ask you about various characteristics mentioned in the text. The list A – L gives the various qualities. Indicate your answers by choosing from the list A – L.

- [ ] 25 What are the characteristics of unrecycled paper? *(3 answers)* ....
- [ ] 26 What is the characteristic of a photocopier? ....
- [ ] 27 What are the characteristics of bicycles? *(2 answers)* ....
- [ ] 28 What are the characteristics of fluorescent lighting? ....
- [ ] 29 What are the characteristics of fertilisers? ....
- [ ] 30 What are the characteristics of plastic cups? *(2 answers)* ....
- [ ] 31 What are the environmental benefits of not going to work? *(2 answers)* ....
- [ ] 32 What are the effects of working from home? *(2 answers)* ....
- [ ] 33 What are the effects of using an ioniser? ....
- [ ] 34 What are the characteristics of slug pellets? *(2 answers)* ....

    A can be used again
    B damages the environment
    C ecologically sound
    D energy saving
    E disposable
    F uneconomic
    G chemical-free
    H a danger to health
    I biodegradable
    J waste-saving
    K we use finite resources
    L saves money

Paper 2 Writing

Section A

You have recently been involved in a minor motor accident which occurred, you believe, through no fault of your own. You filled in an accident report form for the Insurance Company but received a letter back querying some of the details. You feel their remarks are unjustified and that your claim is convincing.

Reply to their letter on the next page, clarifying the points they raised and asking for your claim to be settled as soon as possible.

Use the handwritten notes which you have made on this letter, the outline claim form and the diagram to help you construct your letter.

You may invent any necessary extra details to complete your answer, provided that you do not change any of the information given.

Accident Claim Form

Name: ....

Car Registration No: ....

Make of car: ....

Date and time (approx) of accident: ....

Where it occurred: ....

Name(s) of passenger(s): ....

Names of independent witnesses: ....

....

Damage caused: ....

....

Estimated repair bill: ....

Brief description of how accident occurred: ....

....

....

Exam 3

Dear Claimant,

Thank you for your completed accident claim form dated 25th February. Before any settlement can be reached, however, the Company requires further information on the following points.

1. You state that your rear seat passenger had an unrestricted view of the impact. Surely the driver's head would have been in the way, preventing him from having a totally clear vision.

   [Handwritten note: The other car nearly drove into him – he could see everything!]

2. The lack of an independent witness is somewhat surprising, especially as the accident occurred in broad daylight on a busy main road.

   [Handwritten note: The Olympic Games were on TV!]

3. The extent of the damage to the car is not consistent with the speed at which the other vehicle was travelling. <u>How do you account for this?</u>

   [Handwritten note: Not my fault the other car was built like a tank!]

4. The estimates you have obtained from the two garages seem unacceptably high and we would need to see a <u>breakdown of the figures</u> to ascertain how they were reached before allowing the repairs to proceed.

   [Handwritten note: Cost of labour, parts, tax, have all just gone up.]

An early reply to this letter would be appreciated and could prevent further delays in reaching a satisfactory conclusion to this matter.

Yours faithfully,

Roland Rightoff

Section B

Choose one of the following writing tasks. Your answer should follow exactly the instructions given. You are advised to write approximately 250 words.

1 You have been asked to write a guide to the education system in your country. It would be appropriate to include the way in which the compulsory period of schooling is completed, the types of school (state, private), the selection process (if any) and the opportunities which exist for higher education. Other details such as methods of discipline, the wearing of uniform and the status of teachers can also be considered.

2 A newspaper has commissioned you to write an article describing the appeal of dangerous sport. You should mention a variety of different sports (hang-gliding, off-piste skiing, car racing, etc.) and say what people's motives are for taking part, the potential risks involved, as well as the pleasures people derive from participating in them.

3 As part of a research project on differing lifestyles, you have recently spent a 24-hour period with a person who does night work (taxi driver, police officer, shift worker, cleaner, etc.) to discover what they do when most people are asleep and how they spend their free time during the day. Report on your findings about a night in the day of one of these people.

4 A Travel Company is concerned about a loss of popularity for one of their holiday resorts. You have been asked to go there and describe what a week's stay there is actually like. You should consider the reasons why the number of tourists has dropped (overcrowding, expense, pollution, etc.) and the steps being taken to halt the decline as well as any advantages of going there.

Exam 3

Paper 3 English in Use

Answer all questions from Sections A, B and C.

Section A

1 *Read the article below and circle the letter next to the word which best fits each space. The first answer has been given as an example.*

At the turn of the century, there must have been at least 40,000 tigers in India. No serious conflict existed ... (1) tigers and humans because there were ... (2) forests and grasslands to support both ... (3). And, anyway, tigers were respected. Like the other wild animals and trees, they were ... (4) by the people as an integral part of the environment and had their ... (5) in India's religious and cultural history.

Under British ... (6), tiger hunting had become a popular sport (in 1877 ... (7), 1,579 tigers were shot), but the destruction did not ... (8) to their habitat, and was carried out by an elite ... (9) – the British and the Indian royalty. After independence, in the 1950s, 'hunting agencies' ... (10). Hunters were solicited to take ... (11) in what was described as the world's most exciting sport – the killing of tigers – and they came in their hordes. At the same time, the forests began to be encroached on by a growing population in ... (12) of fodder and fuel. The mass ... (13) of the forests had begun.

There seemed ... (14) hope for the tiger. Then, in 1970, it received a fresh ... (15) of life when Indira Gandhi banned tiger hunting and the export of skins.

  1 **a** of   **b** through   **(c)** between   **d** by
  2 **a** enough **b** plenty   **c** few   **d** much
  3 **a** people **b** animals   **c** habitats   **d** species
  4 **a** created **b** given   **c** regarded   **d** granted
  5 **a** feet   **b** situation   **c** environment **d** place
  6 **a** ruler   **b** rule   **c** ruling   **d** reigning
  7 **a** alone   **b** just   **c** only   **d** lone
  8 **a** extent **b** execute   **c** grow   **d** extend
  9 **a** majority **b** minority   **c** minor   **d** major
 10 **a** flowered **b** fruited   **c** vegetated   **d** mushroomed
 11 **a** place   **b** part   **c** apart   **d** party
 12 **a** destruction **b** increase **c** sight   **d** search
 13 **a** exploits **b** exploitation **c** explosion **d** exhumation
 14 **a** good   **b** few   **c** little   **d** small
 15 **a** time   **b** leaf   **c** lease   **d** purchase

2 *Complete the following article by writing the missing words in the spaces provided. Use only one word for each space.*

Concern for the environment has invaded the consciousness of everybody now. We have all become well aware .... (1) the threats posed .... (2) our Earth by pollution, by the loss of habitats and species and, ... (3) of all, by the destabilisation of our climate that may be brought .... (4) by the increasing output of industrial gases, such as carbon dioxide from motor vehicles and coal-fired .... (5) stations. .... (6) concern has invaded fashion. Rock stars campaign .... (7) the rain forests. Designers .... (8) their clients in ecologically friendly fibres.

But, so far, it has not really made .... (9) felt in the everyday routine of most of us in a practical way. Those who try to put environmental concern into .... (10) in their own homes still tend to be activists, members of pressure groups, people ... (11) level of feeling is .... (12) that of the average.

The coming decade will change all that. The 1990s are certain to see environmental considerations brought forcibly by legislation as .... (13) as by fashion right into everybody's daily lives; in the .... (14) we feed, clean and clothe ourselves, as well as how we heat, light and power our houses. Nothing .... (15) than that will be required as the world community tries to come to terms with the greenhouse effect.

Section B

3 *In most lines of the following text there is one unnecessary word. It is either grammatically incorrect or does not fit in with the sense of the text. Write the incorrect or inappropriate word in the space provided at the end of the line. Some lines are correct. Indicate these with a tick (✔). The first two lines have been done for you.*

Advertisements do appear on everything from beer mats to hot air.	1 *do*
Advertising is everywhere and companies spend billions of pounds to	2 ✔
persuade you to spend on your hard-earned cash. But advertising	3 ...
is more than just about trying to sell products to the world public.	4 ...
It has become an integral part of the everyday life and advertising	5 ...
images affect the way we think and act more than ever before.	6 ...
Research has shown that young people pay for attention	7 ...
to advertising more than anything else on television. A survey of	8 ...
the viewing habits of young people had revealed that over 87 per	9 ...
cent of them rated the adverts the most interesting thing.	10 ...

Exam 3

In most lines of the following text one word is missing. It is either grammatically incorrect to leave it out or needs to be added in order to make sense of the text. Write the missing word in the space provided at the end of the line. Some lines are correct. Indicate these with a tick (✔). The first two lines have been done for you.

Soccer in America

When TV soccer was first launched in United States in the	11 *the*
nineteen sixties, spectators were bemused by the curious and	12 ✔
unexplained stoppages by referees. Three weeks the reason	13 ...
was revealed: the television company which was	14 ...
sponsoring the games had insisted a set number of	15 ...
advertising breaks. Referees had keep electronic devices	16 ...
strapped to their backs that the programme producer could	17 ...
indicate when a commercial was coming up. When the referee	18 ...
heard a 'beep' he had to stop play. However, following	19 ...
number of complaints, the practice was eventually stopped.	20 ...

4 *Read the following fax message from a colleague. Using the information, complete the notice by writing the missing words in the space provided for each item 1 – 14 below.*

John – I've just had the Fire Officer from Head Office on the line – apparently we have to have a notice on all the office doors giving information on fire regulations – could you see to it? You know the sort of thing – the do's and don'ts to stop fire breaking out – like no smoking except in the canteen of course – making sure all the plugs are pulled out at night – knowing where the alarm bell and the exits are – getting out quick if fire starts and where to go and wait until the all clear has been given (the main car park).
The guy is coming round to check the building on Monday, so it's got to be done by then.
Thanks,
Sam

Fire ... (1)
To reduce the ... (2) of fire, the following precautions must be ... (3). Smoking is ... (4) only in the canteen. Make ... (5) all electrical equipment is ... (6) when not in ... (7). Familiarise yourself with the ... (8) in case an emergency ... (9). In the ... (10) of a fire ... (11), vacate your office immediately and proceed ... (12) the assembly area in the main car park. In ... (13) circumstances can you return to the building until it has been declared ... (14).

1	*regulations*	8	....
2	....	9	....
3	....	10	....
4	....	11	....
5	....	12	....
6	....	13	....
7	....	14	....

Section C

5 *Choose the best phrase or sentence (given below the text) to fill each of the blanks in the following text. Write one letter (A – G) in each of the numbered spaces. Two of the suggested answers do not fit at all.*

After 24 centuries the Parthenon still stands on its ancient hill overlooking Athens, a paradigm of Western civilisation, lucid and sublime. (1) ... this masterpiece of classical Greek architecture endured from age to age, from philosophy to philosophy, a symbol of the powers of reason and of the divinity of the human intellect. (2) ... fire and gunpowder, religious intolerance, neglect, vandalism and carelessness ravaged the great temple of Athena, reducing it to the still beautiful but broken fragment that the world knows today. (3) ... , its marble cracking as corrosion weakens iron clamps attached in the early part of this century after earthquakes damaged the structure.

Over the past seven years, the Greek government has mounted a monumental effort to save the Parthenon from further destruction. (4) ... a troubling question has been raised. Researchers have catalogued the debris around the Parthenon and puzzled out its place among the ruins. The temple can be not only preserved but also, to an astonishing degree, reconstructed. Now Greece must decide how far to go.

The issue divides architects and archaeologists, who argue passionately over the aesthetic, scientific and moral wisdom of attempting to reproduce what time has worn away. No one objects to the restoration of the existing structure, endangered as never before by the combined effects of ancient injury and modern pollution. But specialists in the art of the classical period are not at all sure they agree with the recommendation of the Parthenon's chief architect, Manolis Korres, to rebuild most of the pronaos, an interior porch across the eastern end of the temple that has not been there for hundreds of years. Last month, an official committee of scientists recommended that the government accept a compromise: a partial reconstruction of the pronaos that would use over 70% of the original marble fragments together with enough new stone to guarantee stability. (5) ... the government will reconsider Korres' proposal to rebuild the colonnade in its entirety, a far more ambitious plan that would restore much of the temple's antique splendour and would require a larger amount of modern stone.

A Yet over the centuries
B Even as the arguments for and against reconstruction continue
C Even as the world around it changed
D But as modern science has come to the rescue
E The architect's research on the pronaos
F The Parthenon has even suffered from the efforts of those who would save it
G If that proves satisfactory

Exam 3

6 *You have recently returned from holiday in an English-speaking country and feel sufficiently angry about your experience to write to the manager of the travel company to complain and demand your money back. You have already spoken to a representative but she insisted that your comments are put in writing. Before composing your letter you make some notes. Write the letter.*
You must use all the words in the same order as the notes. You may add words and change the form of the words where necessary. Look carefully at the example which has been done for you.

- **a** return two weeks stay Hotel Metropole
- **b** v. unhappy – awful – bedrooms small, uncomfortable and v. dirty
- **c** brochure – all rooms – spacious – spotless – maid service
- **d** also claimed – beach 200m – 10-min. walk away
- **e** v. poor quality food – little entertainment (esp. for children) – as promised
- **f** family disappointed – never again
- **g** compensation appropriate
- **h** otherwise legal action
- **i** regret letter – no alternative

Dear Madam,
I wish to register a serious complaint about a family holiday I purchased from your company.

a *We have just returned from a two-week stay at the Hotel Metropole.*

b ....

c ....

d ....

e ....

f ....

g ....

h ....

i ....

I look forward to hearing from you at your earliest convenience.
Yours faithfully,

Exam 3

Paper 4 Listening

Answer all questions.

Section A First Part

You are staying at your sister's house while she is away on business and realise that you need to use the washing machine but have no idea how it works. You try to contact her but she is too busy to speak to you. However, you manage to leave a message. When you get back from work, there is a message on the answering machine giving instructions on how to operate it. Listen to what she says and complete the instructions.

1 Look at the buttons and ....

2 Where do you press to open the door?
    ☐ E   ☐ F   ☐ G   ☐ H   ☐ I   ☐ J

3 Press the button to release any .... water.

4 Where do you put the washing powder?
    ☐ A   ☐ B   ☐ C   ☐ D   ☐ E   ☐ F

5 Which button do you press to start the machine?
    ☐ E   ☐ F   ☐ G   ☐ H   ☐ I   ☐ J

6 How long does the normal cycle last? ....

7 Advice given if the machine fails to start.
   ....

8 The red light means that ....

Section A Second Part

A friend of yours is planning to take a holiday soon and you realise that a telephone guide service provides advice on what to do before going away. The type of holiday she has decided on is a long-distance package trip to a hot country where she can just swim and sunbathe. She doesn't drive and isn't interested in sightseeing. You wish to pass all the relevant information on to her. Listen to the tape and complete the notes.

   Documents to check:

9 ....

10 ....

11 ....

12 Don't: ....

13 Don't forget: ....

14 Remember: ....

67

Exam 3

Section B

You are going to hear a discussion with a man who believes he has found the secret of making money. He is going to tell the listeners how he did it. You are very interested in his ideas and make notes of what he said. After hearing the text twice, you are able to complete your notes.
Fill in the spaces using a few words. You do not need to write full sentences.

15 He owed money to a .... and his ....

16 When he lost his job his lawyer advised him ....

17 He calls his scheme .... to riches.

18 He wants people to send £10 not because he .... but he wants them to ....

19 What he is actually selling is ....

20 There is no risk because he .... for 31 days after he has sent the material.

21 To make large sums of money doesn't require education, capital .... or .... but it does require ....

22 In order to succeed you must be able to put ....

Section C

In a few moments you will hear various people talking. There are several short extracts which are not related in any way except that everyone has been an eye-witness to an accident or disaster.

23 Below is a list A – G of the people who speak on tape. Put them in order 1 – 7.

☐ **A** a pilot ☐ **E** a tourist
☐ **B** a fireman ☐ **F** a doctor
☐ **C** an office worker ☐ **G** a police officer
☐ **D** a passenger

24 Below is a list of topics H – N. Match each topic with one of the people who speaks. Write the letter A – G beside each topic to show the speaker.

☐ **H** a fire
☐ **I** a car accident
☐ **J** a volcanic eruption
☐ **K** a flood
☐ **L** a hurricane
☐ **M** a shipwreck
☐ **N** an oil-spill

Exam 4

Paper 1 Reading

Answer all questions.

Spyglass on Creation

In the beginning there was the Big Bang ... then there was Galileo ... now there is the Hubble space telescope which, despite problems, may answer man's deepest questions.

1. For the first time in man's life on Earth, the human eye can see images of light from the Creation. It will make possible the biggest single advance in cosmology since Galileo turned his lenses to the sky three centuries ago. The multi-billion-dollar project, which has battled with physical and financial adversity for almost twenty years, should soon repay its supporters with answers to some of the most fundamental questions of existence: when did everything begin, how fast is everything changing, and how long will anything survive?

2. Since it first became a practical possibility in the late 1950s, a permanent telescope in space has been the answer to an astronomer's prayer. At even the highest mountain observatory on land, an obstructive atmospheric cloud lies between the watcher and his quarry in the depths of space. Only the strongest rays get through the gaseous blanket, creating the pattern of planets, stars and emptiness which make up the familiar night sky. These visible configurations, such as the Pole Star, Bear and Plough, form only a fraction of the whole picture. Compared with the prospects from space, conventional astronomy has been likened to bird-watching from the bottom of a lake.

3. A space telescope should see objects fifty times fainter than anything that can be seen by even the best equipment on the ground. The blackness of the heavens will soon be filled with hitherto unseen points of light. That means hitherto uncharted history. As we look into the sky today from Earth, the light from the brightest star, the Sun, is already eight minutes old. We are seeing the recent past. At night, when we look at the next nearest star, the light is four years old. We see the slightly more distant past. The light from the furthest stars that the naked eye can see reflects the world in that part of space as it was two million years ago, when primitive man roamed the Earth. The starlight that the best telescopes on earth can glimpse is very much older, originating up to 10 billion years ago.

4. But, through the lens of the Hubble telescope, in the newly visible fullness of space, astronomers will see in unprecedented detail almost the last step of the way to time's beginning. The light from those furthest stars will have come from the most ancient sources in the universe, from matter that existed at about the time of the beginning of the universe itself. The birthdate of the universe is one of those big unknowns which the Hubble should help to make known. But, according to current estimates, some of the light which should soon land on the telescope's 94.5-inch mirrored lens began its journey 15 billion years ago.

5   It is hard to imagine, but those same light waves, travelling at 186,000 miles per second, were still coming in our direction 10 billion years later, when the Earth that would one day receive them was a mere semi-solid mass of cooling gas. Another five billion years later, those ancient rays of light may finally be measured by men who want to know what it was like when their travels began. This ancient light will soon be refracted, divided, photographed and fought over. There are theoretical problems – and furious scientific arguments – about whether anything visible exists so close to the beginning of time. There have also been problems with certain calculations within the project. But Hubble ought to bring us within a million years of the Creation. It should help reveal the origins of carbon, hydrogen, oxygen, nitrogen, the building blocks of life – on Earth, and maybe elsewhere as well.

Questions 1 – 5

These questions ask you to choose the best title for each paragraph (1 – 5). A – H lists the possible titles. Indicate your answer by choosing from the list A – H and writing the letter against the relevant paragraph number.

Paragraph	Possible title
1	**A** Astronomical figures
2	**B** Breaking through the atmosphere
3	**C** The Age of the Universe
4	**D** Galileo's problems
5	**E** Triumph of technology
	F The light from the sky
	G Stars and more stars
	H Scientists and observers

Questions 6 – 10

These questions ask you to link statements (listed A – G) with things that can be found in space (6 – 10). Indicate your answers to each question by choosing from the list (A – G).

6   atmospheric cloud *(2 answers)* ....

7   light waves *(3 answers)* ....

8   cooling gas *(2 answers)* ....

9   hydrogen *(1 answer)* ....

10 the Sun's rays *(2 answers)* ....

A hinders clear vision   **E** millions of years old

B measures time   **F** travels at speed

C what the earth consisted of   **G** scientists unsure of origin

D visible without a telescope

Exam 4

The ultimate leap of faith

Bungee madness hangs by a wrist-thin line, by David E. Thigpen.

The essence of any sport is to confront a challenge, physical or intellectual, and a twinge of danger often adds to the thrill. But few sports – if this can be called a sport – dare look more closely into the face of death than bungee-jumping, a rapidly growing craze in the US, New Zealand, France and Britain.

As recently as two years ago, bungee-jumping was little known, except to a handful of sky divers, mountain climbers and other daredevils. In recent months, however, a dozen bungee-jumping clubs have appeared and become profitable commercial ventures. So far, an estimated 40,000 jumps have been made in New Zealand, 25,000 in France and 8,000 in the U.S.

Bungee-jumping has one catch: it allows no margin for error. In France, two jumpers fell to their deaths last year when their cords were severed in mid-jump, and a third died after colliding with a tower. In New Zealand two months ago, a man lost his life in a bungee fall.

Enthusiasts maintain that the thrill outweighs the risks. Jumpers leap headfirst from bridges, towers, cranes and even hot-air balloons, from 40 to 100 metres above the ground, with only a long rubber bungee cord to break the fall. Anchored around the ankles or to a body harness, the wrist-thin cord is long enough to allow a few seconds of free fall. Then it stretches and dampens the force of the plunge, sometimes letting the jumper hurtle to within a few metres of the ground. Rebounding to its original length in gradually lessening bounces, the cord jerks the jumper up and down like a yo-yo.

Some participants describe the experience as 'death survived'. Bill Fryer, twenty, an Oxford University student and chairman of a sports club called the Oxford Stunt Factory, has made twenty jumps. Says he: 'You fall incredibly fast. It really wakes you up.' Lance Colvin, (thirty), a computer specialist in Santa Clara, California, is a veteran of fifty leaps. 'The jump is one of the most elating feelings,' he says. 'It's more emotional than physical.' Successful jumpers invariably wear a glowing 'post-bungee grin' reflecting a mix of elation and relief.

Since the sport requires no special skill or conditioning, the challenge is strictly psychological. Veteran jumpers like to tease newcomers by telling them it's not the fall they should be worried about but hitting the ground.

Bungee-jumping originated in a ritual long practised by the 'land divers' of Pentecost Island in the South Pacific archipelago of Vanuatu. Every spring, villagers there collect liana vines and wind them into long cords. Young men then scale high wooden towers, lash the vines around their ankles, and jump. A successful leap is considered a demonstration of courage – and a harbinger of a plentiful yam harvest.

Questions 11 – 15

Below are a number of questions or unfinished statements about the text. You must choose the answer which you think fits best. Give one answer only to each question.

11 What is the essence of any sport?
    a To avoid danger.
    b Not to have to think.
    c To face a challenge.
    d To be thrilled.

12 Bungee-jumping involves
    a cutting a cord.
    b falling into a river.
    c hitting the ground.
    d being suspended.

13 After a successful jump, participants feel
    a sad.
    b sick.
    c happy.
    d tired.

14 The sport requires special
    a training.
    b ability.
    c experience.
    d equipment.

15 The idea of bungee-jumping came from
    a divers swimming under water.
    b students looking for excitement.
    c computer specialists testing a theory.
    d islanders showing their courage.

Exam 4

Shopping is fun

Let me clear up a little misunderstanding. Shopping and buying are not the same thing.

Those who raise their eyes heavenwards and sigh a great deal when others mention that they want to go shopping are buyers. (16) …

Shoppers, on the other hand, are a different breed altogether. Shoppers browse, shoppers explore, shoppers set off on adventures down unknown alleys and uncharted avenues. Quite often shoppers will return home with no purchases whatsoever, or a selection of things that bear no relation to the list they produced before they left, driving buyers (to whom they are usually married) to distraction.

Unfortunately, what buyers will never understand is that shopping is not lining up behind a whole lot of harassed people in a supermarket for a trolley full of pre-packaged food, squashed into submission under plastic. (17) …

Shopping is finding something special, something new and different in some funny, dusty little shop way off the beaten track. It's luxuriating in the atmosphere of some of the world's greatest shopping emporiums; it's trying on a wildly unsuitable evening gown, cut up to here and down to there, and actually entertaining the thought, for all of seven minutes, that you might buy it.

Shopping is fun. (18) …

Top of the bunch, the Grand Opera House of shopping, is Harrods, known affectionately amongst us locals as Horrids, just to show how much we love it. Harrods puts on a bewildering series of top-rated entertainments every day.

The famous food halls, starring the freshest fish, the finest cheese, the best meat and the most succulent fruit and vegetables attract the most loyal audience every day. (19) …

There's the entire ground floor, which displays everything from papier maché trays to pen-holders to pearl earrings.

Upstairs you can lose yourself in the soft, inviting sofas in the furniture department, be dazzled in the Designer's Room, choose a pet, book a set of theatre tickets, have a facial and if you are really a serious person underneath your shopper's disguise, you can do your banking.

Then there's Harvey Nichols, every bit as exciting, but not quite as vast, so you don't get lost so easily. Call it 'Harvey Knickers' to show you know your way around London, and look out for jazzy, eccentric belts and accessories on the ground floor, interesting things to put in your hair and snazzy, confident fake jewellery that is more fun than the real thing, especially for your bank manager.

Selfridges is another top favourite grand hall of shopping entertainment. It's in Oxford Street, so a good bus or taxi ride away from Harrods and Harvey Nichols – time to savour the spree so far. (20) …

And this is only the beginning of the Great London Shopping Experience. There are literally hundreds of other great halls of entertainment waiting to be explored.

Questions 16 – 20

In the passage on the left, some parts of the text have been removed. Match five of the parts of the text (A– F) below with the numbers (16 – 20) which indicate their positions in the passage. Note that one of these parts does not occur in the passage. Write the appropriate letter beside each number.

16 ....

17 ....

18 ....

19 ....

20 ....

A   They are the sort of people who know exactly what they want, where they can get it, and are back home with the right thing and not another single article within half an hour.

B   And there is no city that understands that better than London, home of the best theatre, the classiest productions and the best shopping in the world. Just look at the variety of the entertainment halls.

C   It's crowded, confusing, the entire ground floor smells of the perfumery department, but you can find some wonderful goodies in Selfridges that just don't turn up anywhere else.

D   He glides gracefully with hardly a ripple, from Oxford Street at one end, where it's known (just to be confusing) as New Bond Street, where the shops are sharper, glitzier and newer.

E   They are also the most appreciative. Especially of the part played by the co-stars and walk-ons, mere mortals in straw hats and crisp, white aprons.

F   Neither is it replacing a tired, but much loved sweater with another that will eventually have to be replaced in turn. Nor is it trudging around looking for precisely the same boots Uncle Harry had in 1952, which have stood him in good stead ever since. These errands are chores. Shopping is entertainment.

Coffee: thoughts of a realist

by Robin Young

I have tried it with a stop-watch and I know. Instant coffee is no quicker to make than real. Even grinding from beans takes scarcely more time than opening a jar and, after that, it is just a matter of applying boiling water to powder in both cases. The results are incomparable – yet nine-tenths of the coffee sold in Britain is 'instant'.

It sells, I suppose, on ignorance and laziness. Instant coffee got a head start in Britain because we were primarily a tea-drinking nation, with no strong tradition of coffee appreciation. Even now, many people believe that real coffee has to be lengthily brewed in a percolator, or that it can be kept stewing indefinitely on a hot-plate without tasting brackish.

A restaurant which serves instant coffee would know it risks disgrace, yet thousands are happy to serve real coffee which has been ruined, and it is much more actively atrocious than instant coffee, which is merely dreary.

The good news, though, is that where two-thirds of our coffee imports were of the coarse and inferior robusta varieties and only one-third quality arabicas, those proportions are now reversed. This is mildly encouraging, which is what you could say, too, about the emergence of 'instant' or, more properly, freeze-dried brands such as Cap Colombie and Alta Rica, which are 100 per cent arabica.

There was never much excuse for preferring lower quality coffee, because the price difference on premium grades has always been much less with coffee than they are, for example, with tea or wine. Typically, arabica coffee is only about a fifth more expensive than robusta; even Jamaican Blue Mountain beans, the most famous of all, command about four times the going rate for more common coffees.

But whereas in French supermarkets the coffees have long been clearly marked as arabica, robusta, or as blends of the two, the average British consumer still does not know the difference.

Do not suppose that the recent collapse in the commodity price of coffee, while ruinous for Third World farmers, will necessarily benefit British consumers. The original price of the beans is, in any case, a small element of the final price of the coffee, compared with the mark-ups imposed by dealers, processors, packers and retailers. And while drinking so much instant coffee has little or no effect on the speed with which the cup is ready, it certainly slows up the arrival of any price reductions.

The reason for this is that instant coffee is not a fresh, perishable product but a heavily processed one with a protracted shelf life. Falls in the wholesale price take at least six to nine months to show up on retailers' shelves, if they ever do. This time, the slump in value of the pound may serve to postpone the price reduction indefinitely.

As with most other things, though, there are good grounds for paying more and drinking less. There is medical evidence to link excessive consumption of coffee with headaches, irritability, sleeplessness, and heart disease. And drinking de-caffeinated coffee has as little point as drinking non-alcoholic wine.

Once you start to experiment with coffee it can be dangerously addictive, with so many varieties from so many countries available, so many different degrees of roasting, and so many ways of preparing the final brew. You can spend as much as £500 for an extravaganza of a home espresso, or make do with a spoon and a jug.

My present preference is for high roast Colombian, and I have abandoned the business of detonating the daily blast of coffee by pushing the plunger on a glass *cafetière* for the more instant pleasure provided by an Italian screw-together dual-chambered metal jug which forces the boiling water through a central section, holding the coffee powder, and into the top half for pouring.

I should mention, though, a use for instant coffee. I hear that if you mix it with water to make a thick paste, it is miraculously good as a dressing for cold sores.

Questions 21 – 33

Answer these questions by referring to the article on coffee. Questions 21 – 33 ask you about various characteristics of the types of coffee mentioned in the text. The list A – L gives the various characteristics. Indicate your answers by choosing from the list A – L.

21 What are the advantages of instant coffee? *(2 answers)* ....

22 What is the advantage of robusta? *(1 answer)* ....

23 What is the advantage of arabica? *(1 answer)* ....

24 What are the disadvantages of instant coffee? *(2 answers)* ....

25 What is the disadvantage of robusta beans? *(1 answer)* ....

26 What is the disadvantage of arabica? *(1 answer)* ....

27 What is the disadvantage of decaffeinated coffee? *(1 answer)* ....

28 What are the effects of drinking too much coffee? *(1 answer)* ....

29 What is the main reason for British people drinking instant coffee? *(1 answer)* ....

30 What are the effects of brewing coffee in a percolator? *(1 answer)* ....

31 How is ground coffee similar to instant coffee? *(2 answers)* ....

32 What encouraged people to import good quality coffee? *(1 answer)* ....

33 What often characterises coffee made in a restaurant? *(2 answers)* ....

A quick to make
B good quality instant coffee
C poor quality coffee
D relatively cheap
E relatively expensive
F can cause ill-health
G not fresh
H lack of knowledge
I lasts a long time
J price does not reflect quality
K lacks an essential ingredient
L takes a fairly long time to make

Exam 4

Paper 2 Writing

Section A

At the end of each term, you receive a report from your College giving details of your progress. You feel you have been unjustly criticised in the latest report and make a formal complaint to your Director of Studies.

Reply to his letter, answering his questions and asking for the report to be modified.

Use the handwritten notes which you have made on this letter, the report form, and an outline of the College Rules to help you construct your letter.

You may invent any necessary extra details to complete your answer provided that you do not change any of the information given.

You are advised to write approximately 250 words.

Dear Student,

Having fully consulted your teachers concerning their reports, there are certain matters which require further explanation before I can proceed further. I would be grateful if you could clarify the following points which have been raised.

① Firstly, your attendance at classes has been 20% lower than last term. This is somewhat surprising because, as you are no doubt aware, college rules make attendance a compulsory requirement. Secondly, you have not completed the required **②** number of written assignments and those that have been handed in have been of lower quality. Finally, during some of the **③** lectures you did attend, you interrupted the teachers on a number of occasions for no apparent reason.

Please answer these points, in writing, as soon as possible, as it will enable me to make a better judgement of the situation.

I look forward to hearing from you.

Yours sincerely,

James Squeers

James Squeers

Handwritten notes:
① I've been ill!
② Teachers gave me longer and understood why.
③ Can't we comment and ask questions? I didn't understand!
Not fair! Teachers understand. I did my best.

REPORT FORM

Subject: ....
Attendance: ....
Progress: ....
Written work: ....
Conduct: ....
Test results: ....
Comments:................................
Signed: ....

```
                    COLLEGE RULES
☞ Students are required to use their time effectively by attending
  all lectures, seminars and classes which are part of the
  official timetable.
☞ Written work must be completed as requested and handed in on time.
☞ Respect should be shown to teachers, especially during class
  time.
```

Exam 4

Section B

Choose one of the following tasks. Your answer should follow exactly the instructions given. You are advised to write approximately 250 words.

1. You have been asked to contribute to a book called *The Wonderful World* by writing an article describing the scenery in your country. It would be appropriate to write about areas of natural beauty such as forests, mountains and coasts, and say why they are attractive. Also include places which are typical of your country's environment and less likely to be found in other parts of the world.

2. You have agreed to teach a friend how to play a table game (chess, cards, a board-game, etc.). To help your friend, outline the equipment needed to play, the rules of the game, and what makes it interesting and enjoyable. Also include advice on the techniques to use when playing and suggestions about how to win.

3. Your local newspaper is inviting ideas on the ways in which your area could be improved. Write to the newspaper giving your suggestions. You should include some of these ideas: additional houses, more leisure and entertainment facilities, better transport, parks and open spaces, and ways of attracting industrial development to provide employment.

4. You have been asked to describe your collection (of books, stamps, records, jewellery, etc.) saying how and why you started it, places where the items were bought and any that are particularly interesting or valuable. It would also be appropriate to describe what you would like to add to your collection to make it more complete.

Paper 3 English in Use

Section A

1 *Read the article below and circle the letter next to the word which best fits each space. The first answer has been given as an example.*

There is no alternative!

Britain's drivers are facing a ... (1). They're buying more cars than ever and are fighting for ... (2) space on the comparatively poor road ... (3) . If the environmentalists get their ... (4), many will be ... (5) forced to use public transport. Some Government ministers have also ... (6) they might consider pricing motorists off the road in an effort to cut back on car ... (7). How would drivers ... (8) if they were forced out of their cars and onto public transport? That's the unique challenge a car magazine ... (9) to six members of the same family.

They all lived without their cars for one week and every one of them felt a surge of ... (10) when they got them back. All the people who took part in the experiment suffered at the ... (11) of the public transport system. One of the major complaints ... (12) to cost, in terms of both time and money, when using buses and trains. However, the complaints from the three women in the survey were more serious. They were all ... (13) about travelling on public transport after dark.

Although some undoubtedly suffered more than others, the ... (14) agreed that their freedom and social lives were ... (15) during the week. The younger, fun-seeking ones were unable to travel to discos and to see friends in ... (16) towns.

1 **a** cross **(b)** crisis **c** critic **d** catch
2 **a** limited **b** limitless **c** outer **d** inner
3 **a** netting **b** network **c** web **d** line
4 **a** road **b** system **c** way **d** idea
5 **a** totally **b** politely **c** virtually **d** privately
6 **a** hunted **b** hoped **c** hinted **d** reckoned
7 **a** usefulness **b** users **c** usage **d** sewage
8 **a** try **b** run **c** stand **d** cope
9 **a** charged **b** changed **c** issued **d** received
10 **a** relief **b** pity **c** regret **d** reward
11 **a** heads **b** hands **c** arms **d** minds
12 **a** related **b** married **c** joined **d** engaged
13 **a** easy **b** uneasy **c** difficult **d** delayed
14 **a** partners **b** partakers **c** entrants **d** participants
15 **a** curtained **b** drawn **c** curtailed **d** shortened
16 **a** nearly **b** nearby **c** close **d** bygone

Exam 4

2 *Complete the following article by writing the missing word in the space provided.*

When Greta Garbo died at the age of 84 she had not made a film for almost 50 years. The actress, who .... (1) at 36, spent the rest of her life as a recluse in New York. As she .... (2) so famously in the film *Grand Hotel:* 'I want to be alone.'

Many pages have been written .... (3) her appeal. She played the beautiful but intense heroines that became fashionable in .... (4) Thirties. But she appealed to female audiences just as much as she did to men.

She was born into a poor labourer's family in Stockholm in 1905. Her childhood was .... (5) a privileged nor a happy .... (6). When she was fourteen her father died after a long illness. He was only 48. Two months .... (7) his death, Garbo was already having to work hard for her .... (8). She started work in a department store selling hats. Soon she began to model the hats and to make publicity films. Her first real film role came .... (9) a director spotted her in the street. She then moved to America and .... (10) an immediate success. At the .... (11) of her fame, she was .... (12) a huge salary and a share of the profits as .... (13). However, for reasons which she .... (14) to herself, she gave it all .... (15) and never appeared in a film again.

Section B

3 *In most lines of the following text there is one unnecessary word. It is either grammatically incorrect or does not fit in with the sense of the text. Write the incorrect or inappropriate word in the space provided at the end of the line. Some lines are correct. Indicate these with a tick (✔). The first two lines have been done for you.*

Almost all ~~of~~ the energy used on the Earth comes from the sun.	**1** *of*
Traditionally people used wood as their principle fuel. Trees and	**2** ✔
the other plants absorb energy from the sun using a process called	**3** ...
photosynthesis. It is this energy that is released in a concentrated	**4** ...
form when wood is burnt. More over the last few hundred years we	**5** ...
have come to rely on the so-called 'fossil fuels'. We have grown up with	**6** ...
the idea that they are somehow going to last for ever, rather than	**7** ...
treating them as precious, with a little regard for the future.	**8** ...

Exam 4

In most lines of the following text one word is missing. It is either grammatically incorrect to leave it out or needs to be added in order to make sense of the text. Write the missing word in the space provided at the end of the line.

Jonas Hanway is credited by many with inventing the umbrella. In	**9** ✔
fact Hanway, died in 1786, had seen umbrellas used as sunshades	**10** *who*
in Portugal and brought the idea to London. There, of course, they	**11** ...
were used for keeping rain. But it took nearly thirty years before	**12** ...
he saw them come into general use. This was mainly because	**13** ...
people thought that if you carried an umbrella you were poor to	**14** ...
possess a carriage. However, for some time afterwards, all umbrellas	**15** ...
were referred to 'Hanway's'.	**16** ...

4 *Read the following informal message which you have received from a colleague. Using the information given, complete the memorandum by writing in the missing words in the spaces provided in the list below. The first answer has been given as an example.*

I checked out where we are having our meeting – it's in this place called Doncot – it's a town, not a village, even though it's completely surrounded by fields – about 25km but could be nearer 30km from here. Anyway, the office isn't actually in the centre but sort of on the edge – so go by the main Bristol road and follow the signs for Doncot – when you're getting pretty close keep your eyes open for a sign for Folly Hill. Turn right there – it's easy to spot as there's a kind of tower on a hill – Folly Hill, of course – right where the turning is. If you drive past the tower you've missed it – go back! Anyway – when you've turned right go up the hill and then down the other side – look out for a pub called – surprise surprise – The Folly. The office is about 100 metres down from the pub on the left.

The office is ... (1) on the ... (2) of Doncot a ... (3) town ... (4) 25 and 30km from Bristol. To reach it follow these ... (5). Take the main road to Bristol and ... (6) for the ... (7) to Doncot. About 2km before the town, you will ... (8) a ... (9) for Folly Hill. ... (10) right there. Do not continue to Doncot. You can ... (11) the turning because there is a tower on the hill above the road. Proceed up the hill then ... (12) into the town. The office is ... (13) on the left ... (14) side of the road about 100 metres ... (15) a pub called The Folly.

1 *located*
2 ....
3 ....
4 ....
5 ....
6 ....
7 ....
8 ....
9 ....
10 ....
11 ....
12 ....
13 ....
14 ....
15 ....

Exam 4

5 *Choose the best phrase or sentence (given below the text) to fill each of the blanks in the following text. Write one letter (A – G) in each of the numbered spaces. Two of the suggested answers do not fit at all.*

On the case

I own terrible luggage. This is an embarrassing admission to make in these smart and stylish times. But when I travel I look like a hunchback after a heavy day at the supermarket.

The main problem is my suit carrier. (1) ... my carrier is bottom-of-the-range and has failed to stand up to the rigours of intercontinental travel. The shoulder strap (it has no handle) is made of some slippery man-made stuff which snapped in Geneva Airport a few years ago. (2) ... we managed to make a temporary repair that has seen me through at least fifteen flights. But the repair has made it easy to spot me in the club-class crowd queuing for the extra leg room and free champagne. I'm the hunched one with the shortened shoulder strap praying the staple won't break.

(3) ..., a couple of shirts, some underwear, a few pairs of socks, toiletries, and maybe a spare pair of shoes for that overnight stay in Brussels, Bonn or Bucharest? These are the conditions. The luggage must:

> be compact and light enough to carry onto the plane as hand luggage;
> it must prevent creasing;
> it must stay looking good.

And it must be rugged enough to avoid embarrassing moments when the owner is fighting off other people in the inevitable battle for taxis.

(4) ... . They have a big hook at one end which is attached to a zip-up compartment in which the suits hang from hangers supplied with the bag. (5) ... the bag is zipped and folded in half to resemble a suitcase. The bags differ in size, complexity, price and quality. A designer label can push up the price, but labels are less important than quality. After all, it is not your fellow travellers you need to impress but the people at the other end. You don't want to arrive at your breakfast meeting looking like you have just tumbled out of the drier.

A Once the suits are stored
B Bought in the Eighties
C First you want a handle or strap
D Helped by a baggage attendant with a staple gun
E As the owner of such awful luggage
F So what is the ideal way to carry a suit
G Suit carriers are all based on the same principle

Section C

6 *A friend, who is having to move to England shortly to start a new job with the British company you are already working for, has asked for help in finding accommodation. Before writing your reply, you make some notes.*
You must use all the words in the same order as the notes and change the form of words where necessary. Look carefully at the example.

- **a** found house you look for
- **b** detached – four bedrooms – modern kitchen – garden very untidy
- **c** close to shops – other amenities nearby – office five kilometres
- **d** neighbours friendly – not sure – met only once
- **e** rent quite high – worth it – all facilities
- **f** pay month in advance – also deposit – returnable
- **g** heating, lighting, water not included – paid separately
- **h** easily best seen – especially so close to work
- **i** quick decision required – could lose

Dear Sarah,

I know this is a busy time for you but to help you sleep a little more easily there is some good news from this end.

a *I think I have found the sort of house you are looking for.*

b ....

c ....

d ....

e ....

f ....

g ....

h ....

i ....

I've enclosed a photograph to give you a better idea of what it looks like. As soon as I have your answer I can get on to the agent right away.

Best wishes,

Exam 4

Paper 4 Listening

Section A

A friend of yours is planning to visit Scotland and is interested in doing some sightseeing. While listening to the radio you hear a talk about Hadrian's Wall which was built about 1800 years ago near the border between Scotland and England. As you think your friend might be interested, you note down the details quickly but miss some of them. Fortunately, the programme is repeated the following day so you have a chance to complete your notes before informing your friend.

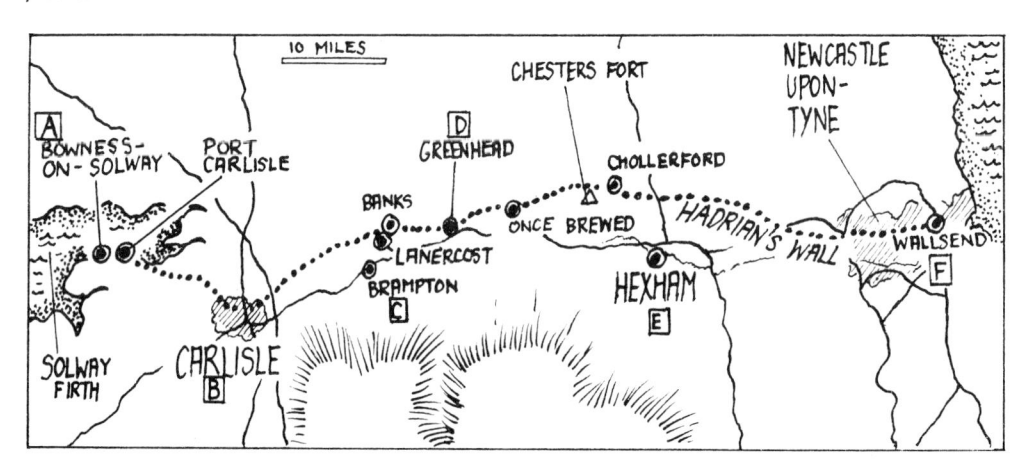

1 The wall was completed nearly ....

2 Where should you start? Tick the correct box. (See map.)

   ☐ A   ☐ B   ☐ C   ☐ D   ☐ E   ☐ F

3 Between Carlisle and Brampton the wall cannot be seen because of ....

4 Where would you go to visit the Roman Museum? Tick the correct box.

   ☐ A   ☐ B   ☐ C   ☐ D   ☐ E   ☐ F

5 Where can you find the best preserved parts of the wall? Tick the correct box.

   ☐ A   ☐ B   ☐ C   ☐ D   ☐ E   ☐ F

6 The best time to visit the wall is ....

7 You are advised not to visit the wall in ....

8 The reason for this advice is ....

Section B

You are going to hear a talk about caravanners and caravanning: how to pull a mini-house behind your car and go where you please. Complete the notes.

9 There are at least .... people who take a caravan on Britain's roads every year.

10 Caravanners do not have to worry about .... for hotels and package tours.

11 The best caravans have .... and ....

12 To pull a caravan you need:

    ....

    ....

    You don't need: ....

13 If you drive a caravan without any lessons you could ....

14 It is against the law to park your caravan ....

    or to leave your caravan ....

15 You must not park on private land without ....

16 The worst problem for other drivers not pulling caravans is ....

Section C

You will hear various people talking about competing in the London Marathon. Question 17 lists the people who speak on the tape. Put them in order 1 – 7. Question 18 lists the things they talk about. Match these topics to the people.

17

- [ ] **A** a roofer
- [ ] **B** an office worker
- [ ] **C** a teacher
- [ ] **D** a housewife
- [ ] **E** a company director
- [ ] **F** a television actress
- [ ] **G** an athlete

18

- [ ] **1** the weather
- [ ] **2** the right clothes to wear
- [ ] **3** collecting money for handicapped children
- [ ] **4** finishing the course
- [ ] **5** the aches and pains
- [ ] **6** the enjoyment of running
- [ ] **7** the prize money

Exam 5

Paper 1 Reading

Answer all questions.

Questions 1 – 5

These questions ask you to choose a title for each paragraph (1 – 5).
A – H lists the possible titles. Indicate the answers to each question by choosing from the list.
What is the best title for each paragraph? Write the number in the box provided.

☐ **A** Taste not waist in the fashion world

☐ **B** It's the customer's choice – or is it?

☐ **C** The fashion revolution – shopping in the future

☐ **D** Making a deal – an exclusive

☐ **E** Counting the quantity, not the quality

☐ **F** Designs on the designers – the risks and rewards

☐ **G** Fair trading – where and what to buy

☐ **H** To buy or not to buy – that is the buyer's question

Clothes

Alix Sharkey speaks to fashion's decision-makers.

1   Every time we shop for fashion, we make choices that tell the world how we feel about ourselves. It is easy to overlook the fact that our decisions have already been limited, framed, *channelled* for us. Not merely by advertising, although that is undoubtedly important. But at a more fundamental level our range of choice has been specified by what confronts us. I mean, how did the clothes get into the shops? They were chosen by a fashion buyer, who has decided, by studying the past and observing the present, what shape our sartorial future will take. This buyer, who must understand the aspirations (and even the pretensions) of his market and cater for them, must also select fashions that will keep his company ahead of the High Street.

2   A nose for fashion, eyes in the back of your head, and one ear to the ground; ask fashion buyers to list the prerequisites for success in their field, and they will conjure up a startlingly surrealistic vision. Having puzzled over what that nebulous entity, the public, will want to wear nine months or a year from now, they reach some conclusion, often based on 'gut feeling'. They hunt down the garments or an approximation thereof, place their orders, then move on, hoping that their judgement will be rewarded. But how can they know what we, their fashion-hungry customers, will want?

3 Some speak in almost mystical tones about their methods, but Jan Stoneham is disarmingly direct: 'I try to see everything. If someone interesting rings out of the blue, I'll always investigate. You never know what they might have.' As Selfridge's buyer of men's designer-wear, her orders must comply with group decisions on the seasonal themes, colours and fabrics. With these in mind, Stoneham visits biannual trade shows in London, Paris, Milan, Florence and Barcelona, looking for suitable garments.

4 Stoneham carries considerable clout inside the business, but there are still occasions when she can't get exactly what she wants, due to the widespread practice of 'exclusivity'. This means buyers placing large or prestigious orders with big-name designers will often demand that theirs should be the exclusive retail outlet for a given area. Selfridges have suffered previously at the hands of Harvey Nichols in this respect, but Stoneham is not discouraged and will persist indefinitely if she thinks it is at all worthwhile. Despite an enormous budget and regular foreign trips, she denies that hers is a glamorous job: delayed flights, hours spent trudging around trade fairs, and the hectic pace of the buying season are some of its least enjoyable aspects. 'It's less than exotic,' she says.

5 A buyer who jealously guards his exclusivity agreements is Peter Fidell, of Jones. He says this is only fair, because he will seek out radical new designers and 'break' them. 'We are always at the front, buying things that are unknown quantities, and the money you invest *before* they are famous is the risk element,' says Fidell, who cites Spanish designer Armand Basi as an example. 'We were the first shop outside Spain to stock that line, and we had it exclusively for a year, but now even shops in my local High Street want to sell it. Exclusivity is important to us, and that's what causes friction.' Fidell says Jones also acts as a shop window for the trade, a fact that gives him leverage when negotiating exclusive rights. 'Buyers from around the country and all over the world constantly come to Jones to see what we stock. I used to say 'Look, you've got to help us because we're going to get you a lot of clients' – but it goes unsaid now. It's understood.

Questions 6 – 10

These questions ask you to identify what factors influence fashion. The factors are listed A – G. Answer each question by choosing items from this list.

A advertising
B trade fairs
C exclusive agreements
D competition
E changing trends
F market forces
G intuition

6 What factors influence customers to buy clothes in the shops? *(2 answers)* ....

7 What factors influence what a fashion buyer chooses? *(3 answers)* ....

8 What factors influence a designer to sell to a particular shop? *(1 answer)* ....

9 What factors influence a retailer to sell different fashions? *(3 answers)* ....

10 What factors influence the range of clothes available? *(4 answers)* ....

Exam 5

Freedom on Wheels

Riding a bicycle is my only claim to being the least bit athletic. I can't swim, play tennis, ski, or horseback ride, but I did learn, albeit with some difficulty, to ride a bike.

What a sense of freedom it gave me, after a long childhood hedged about with anxieties and incompetencies! For I did not master bicycling until the late age of 12. The lack of this accomplishment was such a source of embarrassment to me that, even though I longed to ride and felt that in spite of fears I surely could, I just couldn't bring myself to go through the horrors of learning while running the risk of being observed and mocked by my peers – all of whom had known how to bicycle for years.

In the summer after my 12th birthday an opportunity presented itself. The family went on holiday to the Lake District and there, in a park, were bikes for rent. Since none of my terrifying schoolmates were around, what was to prevent me from learning?

Ever agreeable, and eager to do anything that would get me out of the doldrums of inferiority, my father rented a bike and undertook to help me learn. How he ran up and down the grassy park with me, holding onto the bike and trying to get up enough speed for me to balance myself unaided!

I shall always remember those first few glorious seconds when I realised I was riding on my own and actually balancing. Even though the triumph was short-lived, it was a giant leap forward. From then on, progress was swift, and before long I was even deserting the grassy park for the smooth but forbiddingly hard pavement. By the end of our holiday I was riding reasonably well, if cautiously.

When we arrived home, Dad lost no time in buying me a shiny new bike. Of course it was red – it had to be, to express the extremity of my joy – and the proudest day of my 12 years was the day I ventured out onto the streets with my brand-new red bicycle. Thus began countless hours of soaring freedom, of far-ranging explorations, and of daring feats.

My first accomplishment was going up and down driveways. It was fun to swoop down the incline onto the street and zoom up the next driveway. But soon I desired to emulate my friends, who could all ride 'one-handed'.

This was easily accomplished, but then I was faced with a really formidable challenge: 'no hands'. Finally I had to resort to riding to the outskirts of town where our only real hill was located. Hurtling downhill at a terrific speed, gradually lessening the pressure of my hands on the handlebars until I sensed I really wasn't holding onto them at all, I daringly, with my heart in my mouth, took them away completely, to find myself zooming through the air with a feeling of weightlessness.

After that first year of pure ecstasy, my bike came to be less of a diversion and more of a means of transport. I still have dreams occasionally about hopping onto it and riding down to my girlfriend's house. On arrival I would leave my bike at the foot of the steps, run up onto their porch, and enter the house without knocking, to be met by the warmth of their home.

After an enjoyable evening I would ride silently back through the mysteriously dark streets to our little house, where, from my bedroom window, I could hear the forbidding motorway traffic roaring by.

I've often thought about that red bicycle; it was a kind of turning point in my life. There was a definite emergence from a cocoon of shyness and inhibition into a period of greater freedom.

Questions 11 – 15

Below are a number of questions or unfinished statements about the text. You must choose the answer which you think fits best. Give one answer only to each question.

11 The writer didn't learn to ride a bike until she was twelve because she
   a wasn't athletic enough.
   b was afraid that it would be too difficult.
   c did not have enough time.
   d was worried about the reaction of other children.

12 When she eventually learnt to ride she felt
   a terrified of falling off.
   b inferior to her schoolmates.
   c surprised that it had taken so long.
   d happy at her success.

13 Her greatest achievement was to ride
   a into her neighbours' houses.
   b faster than her friends.
   c downhill very quickly.
   d without holding the handlebars.

14 As she got older,
   a her bike was used less and less.
   b riding her bike became even more enjoyable.
   c her girlfriend was allowed to use her bike.
   d her feelings towards her bike changed.

15 The main purpose of the article is to
   a encourage young people to learn to ride bikes.
   b describe what happens if you don't learn to ride.
   c explain the benefits that learning to ride can have.
   d describe the dangers of riding a bike.

Exam 5

Computers? They're child's play

Walk around a school that educational authorities consider is one of the best. In one classroom pupils are at work on a project on the Black Death. In another, pupils are composing music; in another they are discovering geometry; and a fourth is filled with children chatting. On the face of it nothing has changed. But what is striking is that the pupils are learning with the help of computers.

(16) ... Helped by the computer, the pupils are actively enjoying the subjects they are studying.

In changing the way we live, technology has transformed everything from the factory floor to the high street, and by the year 2000 information technology will be the biggest growth industry in the world. So it's only appropriate that the revolution should have reached the classroom.

'We are no longer talking about computer studies but about information technology', says the schools minister, Alan Howarth. 'IT is a discipline which includes the use of computers and which is part of every subject in the national curriculum now being introduced into schools'.

Parents will recall the drudgery and massive paperwork inseparable from education in even the recent past. (17) ...

In the face of dwindling numbers of school leavers, will today's teaching methods produce the kind of educated young people who will be needed? And, more pertinently, will playing around on computers give our children a good start in life? Or will they do less well than those who went to a school that stuck to old-fashioned pedagogy? (18) ...

In giving 'a central place in the national curriculum' to computers, the objectives are quite clear: that pupils should be able to use IT effectively – communicating and dealing with information, and constructing and solving the kind of problems they may encounter in the real world. Even in infant classes children will be expected to process and retrieve data on a micro. Secondary schools build up to 'more demanding' tasks so that by the age of sixteen or so all pupils should be able to draw, model, compose or improvise using IT and refine as necessary. (19) ...

'Computers can make imaginative work practical', says Ralph Tabberer, Schools Director of the National Council for Education Technology. 'The study of the humanities in secondary schools is a good example. Before computers were available as aids, history and geography were not practical studies. The teacher taught, the pupils made notes. Now pupils can look into stores of data, and analyse what they find'. Involved in this way, 'children have a much more positive attitude to their studies'.

Not least concerned about the impact of computers is the Schools Examination Assessment Council, which is currently investigating IT's effects. SEAC's Madeleine Moore accepts that 'IT will undermine some skills, as the typewriter undermined the practice of copperplate writing. (20) ..., Dr Margaret Cox, head of Educational Computing at the Centre for Educational Studies at King's College, London, is looking into the question. 'The project is still in progress, but earlier research shows great benefits. For example, word processing has a dramatic impact on the way children write – they write for readers, they try to improve their first attempts.'

'Also, IT extends what the pupils can do. In science, for example, they can use simulations to enrich experiments. This is particularly true where observation of actual reactions or processes would be difficult or impossible – such as determining the effect of air density, or shape, on a falling object. It doesn't replace empirical observation and laboratory experiment: it enriches them.'

Questions 16 – 20

In the passage on the left, some parts of the text have been removed. Match five of the parts of the text (A – F) below with the numbers (16 – 20) which indicate their positions in the passage. Note that one of these parts does not occur in the passage. Write the appropriate letter beside each number.

16 ....

17 ....

18 ....

19 ....

20 ....

- **A** But we are producing the citizens of the 21st century, when such skills will be of secondary importance.' IT capability, on the other hand, will be essential. But since there are many traditional skills and abilities that are just as important as understanding IT, does the new education mean skimping on certain basic aspects of learning?

- **B** They should be able to use IT to analyse the requirements for simulating a real system; design, use and test it, taking any legal, financial and environmental factors, for example, into consideration.

- **C** That approach, after all, did well by us and a lot of other people besides. And when figures such as those published in a recent report show that two children in five currently leave school with no passes at the equivalent of O-level, it is no wonder that some parents view the use of computers as just another educational fad.

- **D** Once they had read the novel, they not only wrote their essays on to the screen but used the program's facilities to record songs, draw maps of California and feed in information about other aspects of life at the time of the great American Depression.

- **E** That is what IT frees children from now. Computers are only tools in education, but swifter, more efficient and (as repositories of material) more reliable.

- **F** The history class has stored the parish records of nearby villages and is analysing age patterns and lifespans; the musicians are synthesising the rock music they have just composed on screen; the maths class are moving an onscreen marker through all the degrees in a polygon and pupils chatting are, in fact, having a conversation via electronic mail with friends they have made in schools overseas.

Exam 5

The killers at the bottom of the garden

Along with gardening expert Pat McNeill, we've put together a list that people will find practical. It's not a complete list, but we think you'll understand why we have cut it down.

For a start, we've left potato and tomato plants off the list; although all the parts above ground on potato plants are toxic and all of the tomato plant is poisonous except for the fruit itself. Rhubarb leaves are poisonous though we eat the cooked stalks.

How 'poisonous' a plant is depends on how much of it you eat. A bunch of parsley every day would cause kidney damage, and while one or two apple pips aren't dangerous, a cupful will kill.

The strength of a plant poison varies according to several factors: the time of year; the age of the plant; even the weather. The result of all these variables is that it's difficult to make a single reference list that's really useful. One thing is certain, though, you're right to worry most about children because they have a smaller volume of blood than an adult, and so the same amount of toxins are less diluted and therefore have a stronger effect.

In making up our list, Pat worked from her practical knowledge, realising that it's the colourful berries and seed-heads which so often tempt children to 'taste and see'.

Of course, it's not only children who are at risk of mistaking what is edible. Pat was in the queue at a pick-your-own farm last summer, behind a man who had picked masses of 'blackcurrants'. 'But we don't grow them,' said the mystified checkout girl. The berries were from black nightshade which was growing as a weed among the carrot crop. And yes, the berries are poisonous!

Before you read our list, we've a few general points you should know. One is that packet seeds are often toxic: keep them well away from children. Bulbs and corms may seem perfectly recognisable to you, but it has been known for cooks to use them, thinking they were onions or shallots, with disastrous results!

Don't forget that house plants also have their dangers. Although the castor oil plant rarely produces its mottled seeds, they contain the lethal poison, ricin. Those tempting little orange fruits on the Christmas or Jerusalem cherry we buy at Christmas time are poisonous, and the poinsettia can exude a skin-irrating sap. If the leaves of Dieffenbachia or dumb-cane are chewed they can cause throat swelling and asphyxia. Philodendrons and Swiss cheese plants have similar, but milder, effects.

Pat McNeill lists the plants which are most likely to attract children with their berries, seeds or flowers, and explains what their dangers are.

CHERRY LAUREL: a very common hedging plant, its cherry-red berries appeal to children, but the seeds inside are poisonous. The leaves have sometimes been used mistakenly by cooks because they look very similar to bay leaves.

ELDER: deceptively, the small black berries are safe when cooked and can be made into wine; raw, though, they cause vomiting, stomach pains and diarrhoea.

FOXGLOVE: all the plant is poisonous, including the flowers which children enjoy putting on their fingers.

HEMLOCK, HEMLOCK WATER, DROPWORT and COWBANE: all look like several other common plants that have umbrella-shaped flower heads. Cooked by mistake, their roots and foliage have proved fatal. The philosopher Socrates was made to kill himself by drinking hemlock.

HOLLY and MISTLETOE: even a few berries can cause digestive upsets in a child, but these are rarely serious.

HORSE CHESTNUT: children mistake the conkers for the edible chestnuts from the Spanish chestnut; conkers will cause stomach upsets and vomiting.

LILY OF THE VALLEY: the red berries are tempting but usually make the child so sick that he gets rid of the toxin before it does harm.

SPURGES: sometimes sold as euphorbias. They ooze a white sap when the stems are broken, which can cause a painful skin irritation.

Questions 21 – 30

Answer these questions by referring to the article on poisonous plants. Questions 21 – 30 ask you about various characteristics of the plants mentioned in the text. The list A – L gives the various characteristics. Indicate you answers by choosing from the list A – L.

21 What are the characteristics of cherry laurel? *(3 answers)* ....

22 What are the characteristics of elder? *(1 answer)* ....

23 What are the characteristics of foxglove? *(1 answer)* ....

24 What are the characteristics of hemlock? *(1 answer)* ....

25 What are the characteristics of holly? *(1 answer)* ....

26 What are the characteristics of horse chestnut? *(2 answers)* ....

27 What are the characteristics of rhubarb? *(2 answers)* ....

28 What are the characteristics of lily of the valley? *(2 answers)* ....

29 What are the characteristics of spurges? *(1 answer)* ....

30 What are the characteristics of black nightshade? *(1 answer)* ....

A causes skin irritation
B burns your mouth
C attractive to children
D safe when cooked
E stalks are edible
F causes stomach upsets
G roots look edible but are poisonous
H berries are poisonous
I fruit is not poisonous
J looks like other plants which are safe
K not commonly found in gardens
L seeds are always poisonous

Exam 5

Paper 2 Writing

Section A

You have recently joined your local leisure centre and were asked to complete a comment form giving your views on what they had to offer. As you felt you had some constructive suggestions, you filled it in and returned it.

You have received a letter from the centre which you feel shows a certain lack of understanding.

Reply to their letter explaining what you meant and giving further details of your ideas. Use the handwritten notes which you have made on the letter, the brochure and the outline of the comment form (which you don't need to complete) to help you construct your letter.

You may invent any extra details to complete your answer provided that you do not change any of the information given.

The Leisure Centre
- ☐ fitness training
- ☐ weight lifting
- ☐ squash
- ☐ swimming
- ☐ activities for children
- ☐ refreshments
- ☐ free membership

Comment form

How do you rate the facilities?..

How do you rate the staff?...

....

How convenient are the opening times? ....

....

Other suggestions: ....

....

....

Any other comments..

....

....

....

Dear Member,

Thank you for completing the comment form and returning it to us. The Centre is always pleased to receive constructive suggestions and <u>appreciates the interest</u> you have shown. Before any can be acted on, however, we would be grateful for clarification and further information concerning the matters raised.

[handwritten: I should hope so!]

Firstly, you complained about the 'lack of supervision' in the swimming pool. <u>We would be grateful to know how this affected you.</u> Company policy states that there should always be <u>two attendants,</u> both fully qualified in life-saving, in the pool at any one time. There is also a system whereby other members of staff can be summoned in an emergency.

[handwritten: Being pushed into the water - twice! Chatting to each other with their backs turned.]

Secondly, you suggested that the time when the leisure centre is open should be changed. <u>Could you explain this more fully?</u>

[handwritten: I already have! Crazy to close at lunchtime.]

Finally, you requested that there should be more opportunities for people who do not wish to play sport to benefit from the centre. We appreciate that it is a leisure centre and not a sports centre but would welcome your ideas on the sorts of <u>additional facilities</u> you had in mind.

[handwritten: satellite TV, sauna, jacuzzi]

Thank you again for your response, and we look forward to hearing from you in the near future.

Yours sincerely,

Charles Atlas

Charles Atlas
(Manager)

Exam 5

Section B

Choose one of the following writing tasks. Your answer should follow exactly the intructions given. You are advised to write approximately 250 words.

1 You have been asked to write a review of your favourite restaurant for a food magazine. It would be appropriate to describe not only the cooking but also the atmosphere, the way it is decorated and the types of people who go there. You may also add any suggestions as to how the restaurant might be made even better.

2 A friend has agreed to look after your pet (cat, dog, goldfish, parrot, etc.) while you are away for the weekend. Describe the way you would like it to be taken care of. You should include some information on its habits, how it should be fed, the special treatment it might need and anything else that could make your friend's task easier and more enjoyable.

3 You have been asked to contribute to a magazine article about people by writing about someone you greatly admire. The person need not be famous but should be outstanding in some way. It would be appropriate to write about any special characteristics and achievements which justify your admiration. You should also include some details of their personality and way of life.

4 A newspaper has asked you to report on an event in your area. This could be a sports contest, a local festival, a special anniversary or a celebration. Write about what happens and include a description of the activities which take place. In addition, you should mention how the event might be different in your area compared to elsewhere.

Paper 3 English in Use

Exam 5

Answer all questions from Sections A, B and C.

Section A

1 *Read the article below and circle the letter next to the word which best fits each space. The first answer has been given as an example.*

Human beings have always had the capacity for inventing new products. Some, such as television, have been hugely successful. Others, like a car ... (1) by electricity, have failed to ... (2). As well, there are the simple ideas which, when developed, have ... (3) the inventors very rich. However, in ... (4) to protect the invention, a patent must be taken out. This is a certificate issued to the inventor that gives an exclusive right to the use of the invention. In effect, the inventor decides who can and cannot make, use or sell the original idea. But why patent some of the more unusual inventions? The answer is that you can never tell what might or might not ... (5) people or what might ... (6) to be very valuable at some ... (7) date. Some time ago, a man took a small, smooth rock, put it into a cardboard box and called it a Pet Rock. One could be ... (8) for thinking that this was an extremely silly idea and ... (9) in less than a year he sold over half a million of them.

Then there is the story of John Henry, who decided not to take out a patent on his invention. In 1831, after much ... (10) he found a way to ... (11) electric current through ... (12) of wire and, in effect, invented the first practical telegraph. But Henry decided it would be wrong to benefit from having an exclusive right to his idea. Six years later, Samuel F. B. Morse took Henry's findings, ... (13) on them, and patented his own telegraph. Watching Morse's fortune and ... (14) grow, Henry said: 'Perhaps I ... (15) the situation!'

 1 **a** pulled   **b** dragged   **(c)** powered   **d** fired
 2 **a** catch up   **b** catch out   **c** catch   **d** catch on
 3 **a** made   **b** created   **c** done   **d** earned
 4 **a** command   **b** order   **c** lined   **d** result
 5 **a** integrate   **b** intake   **c** intern   **d** intrigue
 6 **a** turn in   **b** turn on   **c** turn out   **d** turn over
 7 **a** later   **b** after   **c** post   **d** far
 8 **a** forgotten   **b** forbidden   **c** forgive   **d** forgiven
 9 **a** after   **b** yet   **c** since   **d** now
10 **a** discovery   **b** looking   **c** research   **d** science
11 **a** translate   **b** transpose   **c** transport   **d** transmit
12 **a** widths   **b** lengths   **c** sides   **d** poles
13 **a** bettered   **b** improved   **c** stood   **d** pressed
14 **a** fate   **b** flame   **c** money   **d** fame
15 **a** mistook   **b** misplaced   **c** misjudged   **d** mistreated

Exam 5

2 *Complete the following article by writing the missing word in the space provided. Use only one word in each space.*

The Perfect Holiday

British people no longer need to travel to the Mediterranean when they can .... (1) their holidays at home, in perfect conditions, lying beneath exotic palm trees and only stirring .... (2) have a swim or take a .... (3) of a delicious cold drink. It's not .... (4) a dream but just one of the many practical ways to beat the British weather. There is a resort .... (5) people can .... (6) all day sitting around on sun chairs .... (7) the waves lap against the shore, ... (8) the children swim happily or bounce around on an inflatable castle – and no-one ever gets rained .... (9). However, it's not the climate that is guaranteed to .... (10) them dry .... (11) a huge glass dome containing a leisure centre which includes an indoor swimming pool. In the evening .... (12) is live entertainment from a desert island stage and to maintain the theme .... (13) are kept at a minimum of 26°C. Such fully-equipped holiday centres with indoor beaches, tropical plants and waterfalls, as .... (14) as sports and leisure facilities for .... (15) ages mean that wet family holidays spent walking along the seafront can be forgotten. Holiday makers will no longer have to suffer .... (16) afternoons looking at the beach through rain-soaked windows, wondering what to do next.

Section B

3 *In most lines of the following text there is one unnecessary word. It is either grammatically incorrect or does not fit in with the sense of the text. Read the text. Put a line through each unnecessary word and then write the word in the space provided at the end of the line. Some lines are correct. Indicate these lines with a tick against the line number. The first two lines have been done as an example.*

Tobacco is now the most criticised and restricted legal product	1 ✔
in the ~~all~~ world. Blamed for millions of deaths, banned from	2 *all*
many airline flights and public smoking places, its advertising	3 ...
and packaging severely limited, selling tobacco has become	4 ...
the greatest challenge to an advertiser. Nowadays, the few of	5 ...
tobacco's biggest markets are being entirely free from restriction.	6 ...
Although tobacco still generates huge financial profits,	7 ...
promoting and selling it to a growing worried public is	8 ...
becoming more and more difficult.	9 ...

In most lines of the following text there is one word missing. It is either gramatically incorrect to leave it out or needs to be added in order to make sense of the text. Read the text. Put a line where the word should be and then write the missing word in the space provided at the end of the line.

Robots are not all they are claimed to be, at least in the	10	✔
car business. The only clear advantage they have people	11	*over*
is that robots work hours and make fewer mistakes. In some	12	...
ways they are rather a disappointment. Instead of becoming	13	...
better at a task as they get used to it, robots are liable	14	...
to become progressively accurate as the unequal load on	15	...
their mechanical parts wears down bits of them faster	16	...
than others. They are also harder teach and less flexible	17	...
than people.		

4 *Read the following informal message which you have received from your boss, the Managing Director. Using the information given, complete the formal announcement by writing the missing words in the spaces provided below the text. The first answer has been given as an example.*

Do you realise I started this Company exactly ten years ago this coming Saturday? We must have a party to celebrate. Can you arrange the invites – just need to tell people where and when – eightish – that's a bit early – why don't we say nine o'clock at my place. This is going to be something special so it's going to go on until morning – with breakfast for everyone – after all that dancing they'll need it. Tell people not to worry about getting home – I'll do a deal with the local taxi firm – That's about it I reckon – except what to wear – anything they like – I don't go in for all that black tie stuff – and make sure you find out quickly who is actually coming.

Invitation

To .... (1) the Company's .... (2), the Managing
Director .... (3) the pleasure of your .... (4)
at a party to be .... (5) at his home on Saturday next
.... (6) at nine o'clock. As the celebrations will
continue .... (7), breakfast will be .... (8) in
the morning. Taxis will be .... (9) for any
.... (10) who require transport. Feel .... (11) to dress
.... (12). Please .... (13) to this invitation
at your .... (14) convenience.

1	*celebrate*	8	....
2	....	9	....
3	....	10	....
4	....	11	....
5	....	12	....
6	....	13	....
7	....	14	....

Exam 5

Section C

5 *Choose the best phrase or sentence (given below the text) to fill each of the blanks in the following text. Write one letter (A – G) in each of the numbered spaces. Two of the suggested answers do not fit at all.*

From the air, a coral reef stands out as an area of shallow water against the deep blue of the surrounding tropical sea. It is only when you look beneath the waves that you really appreciate its true significance. (1) ... but a living community, one of nature's cities, with its own complex web of relationships. Spires of mushrooming coral terraces and archways surround you and everywhere you look there are fantastic shapes – branching antlers, giant saucers, green boulders, lovely sea fans. It is a surrealistic scene, like a Dali painting.

Darting in and out of these bizarre structures are the colourful inhabitants – an amazing variety of reef fish. Some will flee into a coral crevice as you approach; some will inspect you with idle curiosity; some will simply ignore you and get on with their business.

(2) ..., some of the smaller ones for hundreds of years and others for thousands. There are many types, but it is common to differentiate between three: fringing reefs, barrier reefs, and atolls.

A fringing reef grows up and out from a mainland shore or an island where the sea bed is often of a completely different rock type, such as granite. (3) ...: they coat the ancient continental rock with a layer of limestone.

A barrier reef is simply a fringing reef that has become separated from the shore by a channel usually called a lagoon. (4) ..., is the most famous and most spectacular example. It lies from 10 to 100 miles off the Queensland coast of Australia and is made up of 200 coral-formed sandkeys and thousands of islands with fringing coral reefs. It is 1260 miles long and from 10 to 90 miles wide.

Atolls are ring-shaped coral reefs found commonly in the Indian and Pacific Oceans. (5) ... which at some time or another erupted and rose above the surface. Corals attached themselves to them and a reef developed. If, subsequently, a volcano slowly sank, the only remaining clue to its existence would be an atoll.

A As the corals multiply over thousands of years
B Many were formed around underwater volcanoes
C Australia's Great Barrier Reef, the habitat of countless marine creatures
D The master builders of the reef are coral polyps
E This process is repeated at an ever increasing rate
F This is no mere outcrop of rock
G The reefs we see today have been growing for various lengths of time

Exam 5

6 *A friend has written to ask you for some advice on working abroad. Before writing your reply, you must make some notes. Complete your reply from the notes. You must use all the words in the same order as the notes and change the form of the words where necessary. Look carefully at the example.*

- **a** before leave – check documents – work permit
- **b** health insurance – doctors expensive
- **c** find accommodation – preferably before arrival
- **d** salary – paid in local currency or not
- **e** bank – credit cards accepted
- **f** clothes to take – weather conditions
- **g** travel details and whether met at airport
- **h** differences in local customs and food
- **i** foreign country – feel homesick – natural

Dear Ronnie,

Thanks for your last letter. I'm excited at the prospect of you going to work abroad. You said you'd like to 'pick my brains' as I have some experience of this, so here are a few suggestions.

a *Before you leave, check you have valid documents, especially if you are required to have a Work Permit.*

b ....
c ....
d ....
e ....
f ....
g ....
h ....
i ....

Well, I hope some of these thoughts have been useful. I'm sure you'll have a great time.

Best wishes,

Exam 5

Paper 4 Listening

Section A First Part

A friend is interested in classic and old-fashioned cars, and you hear a radio announcement giving details of an exhibition of these cars. You note down the details quickly, but miss some of them. Fortunately the announcement is repeated shortly afterwards, so you have a chance to complete your notes before phoning your friend.

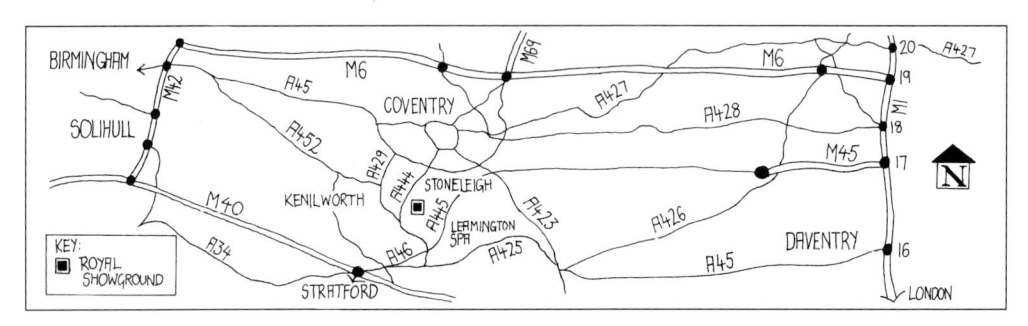

1 The Exhibition will be open on Monday between ....

2 Which is the best road to take if you are coming to the Exhibition from Birmingham?
   ☐ A444   ☐ A445   ☐ A45   ☐ A452   ☐ A46   ☐ M1

3 If you go via Kenilworth you may be delayed because of ....

4 Which road should you take after leaving Stratford?
   ☐ A444   ☐ A445   ☐ A45   ☐ A452   ☐ A46   ☐ M1

5 Which is the best road to take after leaving the M1?
   ☐ A444   ☐ A445   ☐ A45   ☐ A452   ☐ A46   ☐ M1

6 How long is the bus journey from Coventry to the Exhibition Centre?.................

7 What advice is given if you are coming by train? ....

8 How can you avoid the traffic around the Exhibition Centre? ....

Section A Second part

You have just enrolled at a college to do a course which you hope will broaden your knowledge. You will hear a talk given by the course co-ordinator on what you can choose to do. Note down where to meet for the events you choose.
You feel you should spend your time usefully and are not interested in simply being entertained. Your main interests are in science and literature. In the evening you want to relax, but at the same time to feel you are learning something.

Time	Place	Event
Morning	9	10 ....
Afternoon	11	12 ....
Evening	13	14 ....

Exam 5

Section B

You are going to hear a talk on the nature of things: how objects can sometimes appear to come to life. Answer the questions.

15 What do the rocks in California's Death Valley appear to do?

....

16 What was strange about the computer in the North of England?

....

17 What three other objects appear to come to life?

....

18 What might be the views of conventional scientists on these theories?

....

19 What two things are mentioned which suggest computers have minds?

....

20 According to the writer machines will finally make human beings ....

and ....

21 What might happen if you ask a computer to give an opinion of this book?

....

22 The most irritating thing a vending machine does to a human being is

....

Section C

In a few moments you will hear some different people talking. They are on a round-the-world cruise and they are talking about why they are there. Question 23 lists the people who speak on the tape. Put them in order 1 – 7. Question 24 lists the things they talk about. Match these topics with the people. Write the appropriate letter A – G in each box.

23
- ☐ **A** a doctor
- ☐ **B** a bank manager
- ☐ **C** a retired lady
- ☐ **D** an actress
- ☐ **E** a parent of young children
- ☐ **F** a honeymooner
- ☐ **G** an ex-sailor

24
- ☐ the sea
- ☐ the food
- ☐ the entertainment
- ☐ the sights
- ☐ seasickness
- ☐ meeting people
- ☐ peace and quiet

Exam 1

Paper 5 Speaking

CANDIDATE ONE

1 *The examiner will ask you to describe the photograph below to your partner, who has a photograph which is related to yours in some way.*
At the end of one minute the examiner will ask your partner to say what the relationship between your pictures is. You should then try to reach agreement with your partner.

Exam 1

CANDIDATE TWO

1 *The examiner will ask your partner to describe a photograph to you. The photograph below is related to your partner's in some way. At the end of one minute, you should listen and ask short questions if you wish / if necessary. The examiner will ask you to say what the relationship is between the photographs. You should then try to reach agreement with your partner.*

Exam 1

CANDIDATE ONE

2 *The examiner will ask your partner to describe one of the six scenes below to you. It is the street where he or she is staying in England. At the end of one minute the examiner will ask you to say which photograph your partner was describing.*

CANDIDATE TWO

2 *Choose the street you are staying in while you are in England. The examiner will ask you to describe it to your partner (who has the same six photographs). At the end of one minute the examiner will ask your partner to identify your street.*

Exam 1

CANDIDATES ONE AND TWO

3 *Below are the finalists' drawings in a children's competition. They had to draw a picture of their ideal home. (Your partner has the same pictures.) Discuss with your partner which is the winner and why. You must either reach agreement or 'agree to disagree'. Make sure that you understand your partner's opinion. At the end of three minutes you will be asked to report your decision to the examiner.*

Paper 5 Speaking

Exam 2

CANDIDATE ONE

1 *The examiner will ask you to describe the photograph below to your partner, who has a photograph which is related to yours in some way.*
At the end of one minute the examiner will ask your partner to say what the relationship between your pictures is. You should then try to reach agreement with your partner.

Exam 2

CANDIDATE TWO

1 *The examiner will ask your partner to describe a photograph to you. The photograph below is related to your partner's in some way. At the end of one minute, you should listen and ask short questions if you wish/if necessary. The examiner will ask you to say what the relationship is between the photographs. You should then try to reach agreement with your partner.*

Exam 2

CANDIDATE ONE

2 *Do not look at the diagram below. In the examination itself, you will not be able to see it.*

Take a pencil or pen and a blank piece of paper. Draw a simple diagram exactly as your partner tells you to.

CANDIDATE TWO

2 *Look at the diagram. Your partner has a pencil or pen and a blank piece of paper. Give instructions so that he or she can draw a diagram exactly the same as the one you are looking at.*

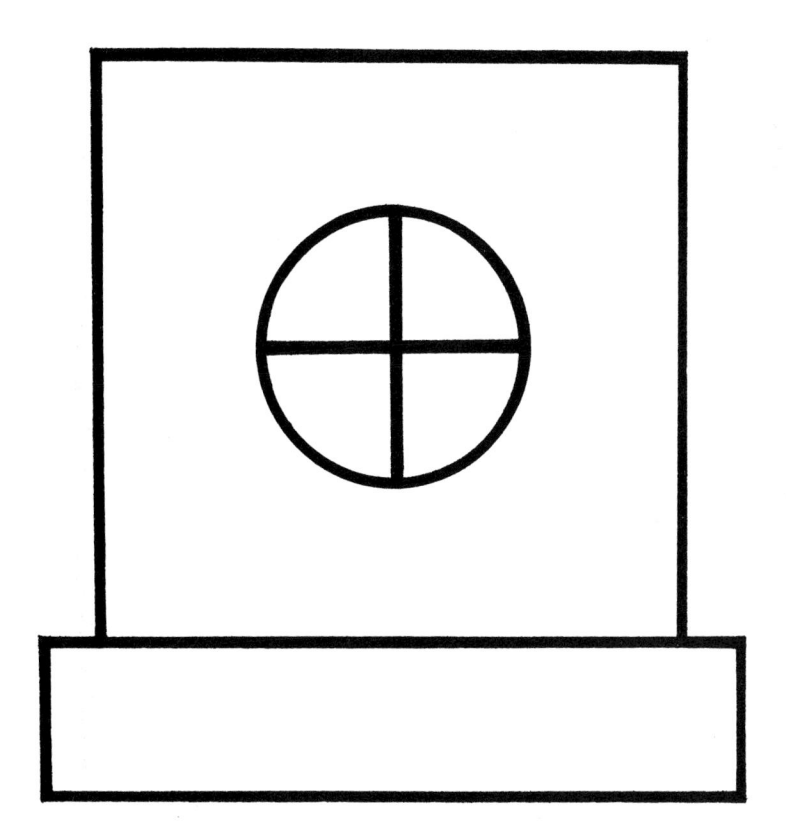

Exam 2

CANDIDATES ONE AND TWO

3 *Look at the two photographs below. (Your partner has the same photographs.) Discuss with your partner which is more beneficial for children: a traditional and relatively strict approach to education or a more relaxed one. You must either reach agreement or 'agree to disagree'. Make sure that you understand your partner's opinion. At the end of three minutes you will be asked to report your decision to the examiner.*

Exam 3

Paper 5 Speaking

CANDIDATE ONE

1 *The examiner will ask you to describe the photograph below to your partner, who has a photograph which is related to yours in some way.*
At the end of one minute the examiner will ask your partner to say what the relationship between your pictures is. You should then try to reach agreement with your partner.

115

Exam 3

CANDIDATE TWO

1 *The examiner will ask your partner to describe a photograph to you. The photograph below is related to your partner's in some way. You should listen and ask short questions if you wish / if necessary. At the end of one minute, the examiner will ask you to say what the relationship is between the photographs. You should try to reach agreement with your partner.*

Exam 3

CANDIDATE ONE

2 *The examiner will ask your partner to describe the most dangerous office scene to you. At the end of one minute, the examiner will ask you to say which office your partner was describing.*

CANDIDATE TWO

2 *Choose the most dangerous office below. The examiner will ask you to explain why it is so dangerous to your partner (who has the same three pictures). At the end of one minute, the examiner will ask your partner to say which office you were describing.*

Exam 3

CANDIDATES ONE and TWO

3 *Look at the two photographs below. (Your partner has the same photographs.) Discuss with your partner which of these two people gets most out of life and why. You must either reach agreement or 'agree to disagree'. Make sure that you understand your partner's opinion. At the end of three minutes you will be asked to report your decision to the examiner.*

Exam 4

Paper 5 Speaking

CANDIDATE ONE

1 *The examiner will ask you to describe the photograph below to your partner, who has a photograph which is related to yours in some way.*
At the end of one minute the examiner will ask your partner to say what the relationship between your pictures is. You should then try to reach agreement with your partner.

Exam 4

CANDIDATE TWO

1 *The examiner will ask your partner to describe a photograph to you. The photograph below is related to your partner's in some way. You should listen and ask short questions if you wish / if necessary. At the end of one minute, the examiner will ask you to say what the relationship is between the photographs. You should try to reach agreement with your partner.*

Exam 4

CANDIDATE ONE

2 *Do not look at the plan below. In the examination itself, you will not be able to see it.*

Take a pencil or pen and a blank piece of paper. Draw the plan exactly as your partner tells you to.

CANDIDATE TWO

2 *Look at the plan of a park below. Your partner has a pencil or pen and a blank piece of paper. Brief him or her so that he or she can draw the plan exactly as it is shown here.*

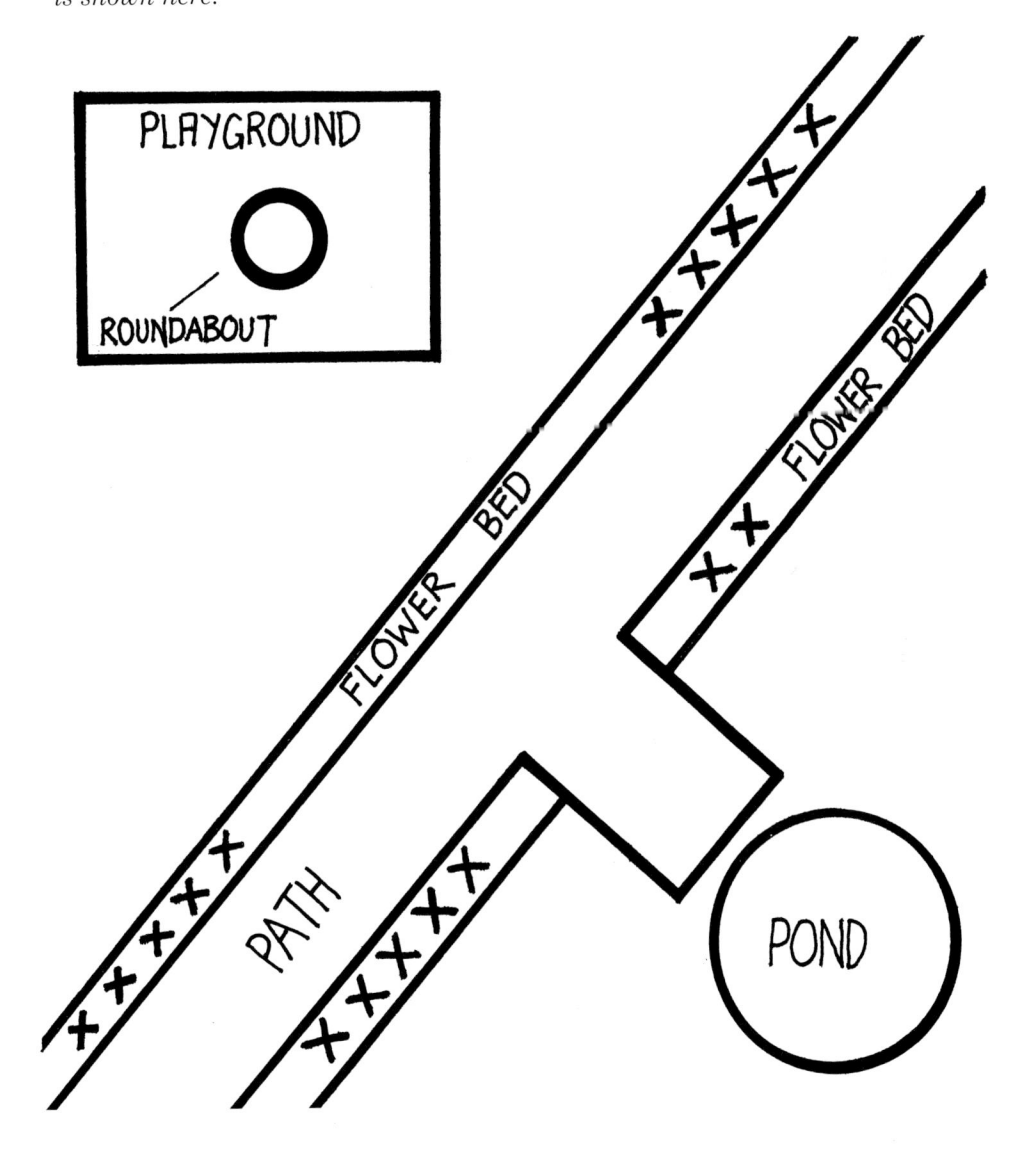

Exam 4

CANDIDATES ONE AND TWO

3 *Look at the two photographs below. (Your partner has the same photographs.) Discuss with your partner which holiday you would prefer and why. You must either reach agreement or 'agree to disagree'. Make sure that you understand your partner's opinion. At the end of three minutes you will be asked to report your decision to the examiner.*

Exam 5

Paper 5 Speaking

CANDIDATE ONE

1 *The examiner will ask you to describe the photograph below to your partner, who has a photograph which is related to yours in some way.*
At the end of one minute the examiner will ask your partner to say what the relationship between your pictures is. You should then try to reach agreement with your partner.

Exam 5

CANDIDATE TWO

1 *The examiner will ask your partner to describe a photograph to you. The photograph below is related to your partner's in some way. You should listen and ask short questions if you wish / if necessary. At the end of one minute, the examiner will ask you to say what the relationship is between the photographs. You should try to reach agreement with your partner.*

Exam 5

CANDIDATE ONE

2 *The examiner will ask your partner to describe one of the six photographs below to you. At the end of one minute, the examiner will ask you to say which photograph your partner was describing.*

CANDIDATE TWO

2 *The examiner will ask you to describe one of the six photographs below to your partner (who has the same pictures). At the end of one minute the examiner will ask your partner to say which photograph you were describing.*

Exam 5

CANDIDATES ONE AND TWO

3 *Look at the two pictures below. (Your partner has the same pictures.) Discuss with your partner which life is better for animals and why. You must either reach agreement or 'agree to disagree'. Make sure that you understand your partner's opinion. At the end of three minutes you will be asked to report your decision to the examiner.*